FROM OLD GUARD
TO VANGUARD:
A SECOND GENERATION PANTHER

MALIK ISMAIL

9/23/2016 2:30:47 PM

1

Printed in the United States of America

Acknowledgments

This book would not have been possible without the love, support and integral roles that have been played by many.

Therefore, I express dedication and thanks to the following:

I thank my mother, Vera, and wife, Kathy, who inspired me. Thanks to my mentor and comrade Charles "Boko" Freeman, along with my longtime comrade and friend Kamau Osiris, they remain consistent friends during my ups and downs. I dedicate this book to my comrades in the New Panther Vanguard Movement, who served the people with me during our time.

To Shareef Abdullah and B. Kwaku Duren for allowing me to serve the people in an organization best fitted for me. To Billy X Jennings of the It's About Time Alumni Committee, who keeps the remembrance of the Black Panther Party (BPP) alive. I would like to thank Billy for letting me work on the BPP reunions, conferences, photo exhibits, and all associated efforts. To our comrades in the Black Panther Collective (BPC), Brown Berets, American Indian Movement, the Young Lords vets, National People's Campaign, our Vanguard chapters in L.A., Indianapolis and Atlanta with Nahylah, Barufo, Kambui, Lutlao, and others who worked with both the Indianapolis and Atlanta chapters making it truly a national organization.   To the first generation of Black Panther Party members who saw our work in the community and declared that we were a part of the legacy; to Bobby Seale and Huey P. Newton for teaching us that, "The spirit of the people is greater than the man's technology".   To former Los Angeles Black Panther member Ronald Freeman, who was a great voice of wisdom to me and other Vanguard members during my Los Angeles "Panther" days. To Wayne Pharr, Roland Freeman (Ronald's brother), Brother Yusef, and other first generation Los Angeles Black Panther Party members who supported and served as great mentors to all Vanguard members during our era. To the Anderson and Lemelle families for their support and love.

A special thanks goes to Goodie Williams: I am glad you were an example for me instead of me being an example for you. To my sister, Mia, who showed me a lot more of the world than I expected and always supported me. To Thomas Hall, author of "ANU America" for encouraging me to write a book. To my grandfather, Jarrot Anderson Sr., who showed me the example of a real man. Finally, an extra special thanks goes to the three icons in my life: Malcolm X and Muhammad Ali, who made me proud to be a Black man, and to the Black Panther Party for making me proud to be a human being. – Malik Ismail

Inspiration Quotes

"To die for the racists is lighter than a feather, to die for the people is heavier than any mountain and deeper than any sea". By having no family, I have inherited the family of humanity. By having no possessions, I have possessed all. By rejecting the love of one, I have received the love of all. By surrendering my life to the revolution, I found eternal life".

>   *Huey P. Newton*

"You don't fight racism with racism; the best way to fight racism is with solidarity". "When donors visited the Black Panther Party, they came and saw our real programs, a real clinic, with real doctors and medics, giving service to the people".

>   *Bobby Seale*

"Are we the same as the Party that Huey P. Newton and Bobby Seale started? No, thirty years have passed, they were in the sixties, we're in the nineties, in fact that was thirty years ago from where we are at today, so our program, necessarily, must reflect the concrete conditions of our time and situation right now, just like the original Black Panther Party reflected the time and condition in 1966".

>   *Shareef Abdullah, Co-founder of the NPVM with B. Kwaku Duren*

"A Platform without a Program is Symbol without Substance and a Program without a Platform is a Charity".

"Malcolm X and Muhammad Ali made me proud to be a Black Man, the Black Panther Party made me proud to be a Human Being".

Malik Ismail

To Our Fallen Comrades:

Panther Vanguard's Shareef Abdullah, Hanif Mack, and sister Loretta Dillon from Indianapolis as well as our Los Angeles Black Panther Party mentors and supporters Ronald and Roland Freeman, Wayne Pharr, and L.A. Panther martyrs John Huggins and Bunchy Carter – Rest in Power (RIP)

TABLE OF CONTENTS

Introduction by Charles "Boko" Freeman

A general overview of the birth of the New Panther Vanguard Movement as experienced by Malik Ismail, a young revolutionary journalist in Los Angeles during the mid-1990s. Malik presents a personal and insightful analysis of important events that helped shape him as a young writer and activist. More importantly, Malik reveals the link between the original Black Panther Party and the New Panther Vanguard Movement as illustrated in their commitment to community service, collaboration with other social justice organizations. The New Panther Vanguard Movement originated in Los Angeles in 1994, and similar to the Black Panther Party, the organization was rooted in community service and the pursuit of social justice.

Malik's narrative chronicles his participation in New Panther Vanguard Movement and how his relationship with founding members, Shareef Abdullah, Kwaku Duren, and myself Charles "Brother Boko" Freeman inspired him to a life of service to others. I first met Malik in Leimert Park at the introduction of the organization to the Los Angeles community. The event included various speeches and a major food giveaway. Impressed by the organization's mission Malik came to study, and later joined NPVM. As comrades, Malik and I organized rallies and events in Los Angeles. He soon relocated to Georgia where he continued to write. In 2005, I relocated to Georgia and we re-connected building upon a friendship established in community service some years ago.

Malik narrates a story of community and political action rooted in the powerful legacy of the Los Angeles chapter of the Black Panther Party. He documents the history of a related organization that served the communities of south central Los Angeles in the mid-1990s. It is my hope that through Malik's work, other researchers will continue to explore and document the far-reaching influences of the original Black Panther Party.

All Power to the People! –

Charles "Brother Boko" Freeman

July 2016

MISSION

The purpose for writing this book is to make a clear distinction that the legacy of the Black Panther Party was carried on in the hearts and minds of the New Panther Vanguard Movement, who, like the original Black Panther

Party, "Served the People – Body and Soul". Mumi Abu Jamal was quoted in the book, "Liberation, Imagination, and The Black Panther Party" stating there are different Black Panther legacy perspectives – successor and competitor. The New Panther Vanguard Movement in Los Angeles and the Black Panther Collective in New York were considered successors. The African People's Socialist Party and the National People's Democratic Uhuru Movement are considered competitors. I believe the New Black Panther Party is considered an imitator." These various perspectives can impact the historical legacy of the original Black Panther Party.

A platform without a program is symbol without substance. Some groups were all image and platform but lacked a program of substance to make an impact in the community other than the media interest and the Million Man March-style gun parades after the fact of a crime.

The legacy of the Black Panther Party needs to be respected and protected for the good that they did in the community and the world as the vanguard of the revolution from the perspectives of African Americans and the people overall. To serve the media instead of the very community from whence you have come is not carrying this legacy forward. The Black Panther Party's co-founder, Huey P. Newton, was quoted, "There are those that only want to be known in the media but can best be judged by establishing survival programs – pending revolution". The original Black Panther Party, New Panther Vanguard Movement in L.A., and the Black Panther Collective New York were not hate groups, but the other groups seemed (by their rhetoric) to be vehemently anti-White in their sentiment and lacked community base programs, which made them little more than image-jacking "hair and nail shop revolutionaries". In other words, they were only interested in the superficial, external beauty of the BPP imagery.

While I like what the Detroit New Black Panther Party did by handing out free water to the Flint community during the water crisis, the national New Black Panther Party has no continuous programs for the people and is composed of many former members of the Nation of Islam who followed Dr. Khalid Adbul Muhammad out of the Nation of Islam along with eager youngsters who want to assume the powerful image of the original Black Panther Party without programs, violent rhetoric, and having no interest in non-racial coalitions. They are more New Black Muslim Movement than Black Panther Party if looked at closely.

THE BLACK PANTHER LEGACY

Birth Of A
Second Generation Panther

Standing on a platform at Leimert Park in Los Angeles, I found myself next to Civil Rights icon Jesse Jackson and United States Congresswoman Maxine Waters, who spoke after me in support of Mumia Abu Jamal. In addition, speaking on the platform that day was radio personality Casey Kasem of "American Top 40" fame and actor Ed Asner. Actress Lisa Bonet (of the Cosby Show) and many others were in attendance. Mr. Jamal was scheduled to die after Philadelphia Mayor Tom Ridge signed the death warrant to proceed with his execution. Mr. Jamal was an award-winning journalist, a John Africa supporter, former Philadelphia Black Panther member, and a globally recognized political prisoner convicted of the murder of Philadelphia police officer Daniel Faulkner in 1981. Mumia was on trial for first-degree murder, convicted by a jury on July 3, 1982, and subsequently sentenced to death. Sitting Judge Albert F. Sabo had a reputation for exclusively hearing homicide cases. Judge Sabo presided over 31 cases that resulted in the imposition of the death penalty.

Less than two years earlier, I worked the graveyard shift as a security guard for American Honda in San Pedro, California. During the day, I attended Los Angeles Harbor College as a student. I remember looking at "brothers" wearing the image of Malcom on t- shirts as I stood in a long line at the movie theatre with my girlfriend Kathy to watch a Spike Lee movie starring Denzel Washington aptly named "Malcolm X". I decided to go to the Eso Won Book Store in Baldwin Hills and purchase "*The Autobiography of Malcolm X* " by Alex Haley, which now remains the most influential book in my life.

In 1994, I fulfilled a lifelong dream of mine to go to Africa. This was a year after my father, James Robinson, Sr. died, who first inspired me to go after a question I asked him on a beach in Miami as a youngster. As my father and I were looking at the ocean, I turned to him and asked, "Daddy, what's on the other side of that water?"

He turned to me and said, "Africa."

It was not what he said to me that stayed with me; it was the way he said it that would spark my interest into going one day. The pride elicited in his tone was invoking. A few generations earlier, if you called any Black person an African or said they were from Africa, you could find yourself in a fistfight. The mass media stereotyped Africa as a place with savages; they portrayed us as people with bones in our noses with no culture until the arrival of Europeans, who arrived to "civilize the natives on the Dark Continent." Those times were a far cry from me standing with my "dashiki wearing" father with immense Black pride. At the time, I was visiting from Louisiana (where my sister Mia and I lived with our mother, who divorced my father after seven years of marriage). What led me to standing on this stage other than reading the *Autobiography of Malcolm X* and my reaction to my father's pride in the African homeland was meeting Stokely Carmichael, then known as "Kwame Ture," while attending a conference in Ghana. Meeting Stokely was thrilling, and he shared a piece of advice that stayed with me the entire time I was in Ghana and upon my return to the United States. He asked if I was a part of any organization. I admitted I was not, and he challenged me on the spot to join some positive Black organization that worked for the betterment of the Black community. Stokely told me to dedicate at least one day a week to serve my people was a small sacrifice of time, considering the struggle our people have had in what he called "Babylon." One of Stokely Carmichael's greatest quotes was, "If your people are oppressed and you are not making a contribution to end the suffering of your people, by your very act of inaction, you are against your people. There is no middle ground".

Upon my return, I had the task of looking for an organization to join that would be a good fit for me. I remember reading about all the Black organizations that were considered influential in the Black community such as Congress of Racial Equality (CORE), National Association for the Advancement of Colored People (NAACP), The Urban League, various Black Nationalist groups, Nation of Islam, and other organizations that I considered becoming a part of. The problem was that none of these organizations solved the problems of the grassroots or "brothers on the block" without the cultural and spiritual nationalism that came up short in regards to a collective programmatic approach. Had I been born a few generations earlier and if Malcolm X had lived, I certainly feel I would have joined Malcolm's Organization of Afro American Unity (OAAU), which he modeled after the African-based Organization of African Unity (OAU). The question for me was since there was no OAAU, who were the children or heirs to Malcolm X? The answer was The Black Panther Party for Self Defense, which was organized by Huey P. Newton and Bobby Seale in Oakland, California on October 15, 1966. I was aware enough to know that the original Black Panther Party was started in 1966 and was defunct by 1981, so I concluded that I needed to find a "Panther-like" organization or the nearest thing to one.

A week after I arrived back in Los Angeles from Africa, I happened to pick up a flyer advertising an event at the Marla Gibbs Theater in Los Angeles. The event was hosted by the New African American Vanguard Movement (NAAVM) and was advertised as Remembering the Black Panther Party, Festival and Forum. Also, there would be a moving tribute to Los Angeles Black Panther Alprentice "Bunchy" Carter, who was assassinated by agents within the US Organization along with John Huggins at the University of California Los Angeles (UCLA) campus. Nora Carter, "Bunchy" Carter's mother, was honored at the event held on October 15, 1994. Prior to the event, I called the number on the flyer and spoke with Shareef Abdullah, who was a young member of the original Black Panther Party from 1976-1981 under the leadership of B. Kwaku Duren, Chairman of the Southern California Black Panther Party. Shareef was very warm and encouraging when we spoke, so I became very excited to not only meet him but the rest of the "New Panther" group. I would learn the name of each presenter who represented the New African Vanguard Movement including Goodie Williams, Kizzy Brown, David

Ingram, and a few others as the event went along. After all that I had been through in finding a good fit for me organizationally, it felt like finding a woman that I had been dreaming about without ever looking at her, but I knew what she could do for me. Once I finally saw "her," it was instant love. That is how I would describe my first introduction to the New African Vanguard Movement. This is how my journey into becoming a second generation Panther began. Certainly, any member of the Black Panther Party knows that the influence of the Lowndes County Freedom Organization, Robert Williams, and the Deacons for Defense inspired Huey P. Newton and Bobby Seale to organize the Black Panther Party for Defense, but it began with Malcolm X – The Progenitor Panther who the Black Panther Party starts its chronology!

Malcolm X:
The Progenitor Panther

"If they had not murdered Malcolm X, there probably never would have been a Black Panther Party."

- Bobby Seale,
Co-founder of the Black Panther Party

The 50th Anniversary of the Black Panther Party will be celebrated October 2016 in Oakland, California, where it all began. However, the Black Panther Party starts its chronology at the assassination of Malcom X, which was 51 years ago this past February 21st. Soon, we will be celebrating what would have been Malcolm's 91st birthday had he lived. These two controversial influential entities would leave a lasting impression for generations to come along with a legacy of activism: Malcolm and the children of Malcolm!

The definition of a progenitor is an ancestor in direct line or a forebear. Bobby Seale and Huey P. Newton, cofounders of the Black Panther Party, both said that the nature of the panther is an animal that when driven into a corner and it can't go left or right, it will come out of that corner to destroy its enemy absolutely and completely. In *The Autobiography of*

Malcolm X, writer M. S. Handler wrote in the introduction about the reaction of his wife to Malcolm after having invited him to their home and serving him tea while he discussed the book with her husband. Handler described what she thought of Brother Malcolm after he departed their residence in these words, "You know, it was like having tea with a Black Panther." Mr. Handler thought about that description and concluded that the black panther animal is an aristocrat in the animal kingdom. Like Malcolm, the panther is beautiful and dangerous. As a man, Malcolm X had the bearing of a born aristocrat and was potentially dangerous to the White power structure. No man of our time aroused as much fear and hatred from the White man as Malcolm X because, in him, the White man sensed an implacable foe who could not be had for any price. Black people, like a cornered black panther, have had our collective backs against the walls of oppression by White supremacy, imperialism and colonization. Brother Malcom was the one who came out of that corner to confront the enemy of his people.

Malcolm X was always quoted as saying, "History is best qualified to reward all research." When studying the history of Black people in America in dealing with oppression of the power structure, he saw the necessity for our people to strike back against our oppressors in self-defense and selfdetermination. Because of the oppression, repression, and psychological warfare of self-hate, we have seen ourselves as inferior and not worthy of confronting the reactionary racists at any level of society in a systematic social order enforced system. Behind closed doors, Civil Rights leaders like Martin Luther King, A. Phillip Randolph, Whitney Young, Roy Wilkins, and others would use Malcolm's defiant words as a "counter" to them in order to obtain civil rights cooperation from the power structure. Those leaders would tell government officials, "Look, we are non-violent. But outside is that other brother, and he is not like us". United States officials would be more flexible in their positions and more willing to negotiate with the civil rights leaders or eventually be confronted by Malcolm X – The Progenitor Panther. The Civil Rights leaders' main emphasis was based on the morality of having an equal society for all to bring about social change. Malcolm and later the Black Panther Party knew that the system's opposition had nothing to do with mortality but everything to do with power in a one-sided Capitalistic social order.

The Black Panther Party would declare, "All power to the people," and organized the people in direct opposition to the power structure. This proved to be the best way to empower the powerless of all the people in an oppressive system. Peter Bailey, a close aide to Malcolm, recalled, "Brother Malcolm was one of the first people I heard talking about the system. He never said, 'It's the George Wallace types.' Brother Malcolm said, Oh, no. We are talking about the whole system." Malcolm would lance our sense of inferiority because he felt like our people do not think much of themselves or their history will not have the confidence to fight for their rights as equal citizens. Alex Haley, who wrote Malcolm's autobiography, was startled by a statement Malcolm made about himself when he told Alex, "I am a part of all I have met," meaning that everything he had encountered in his life had synopsized into the Malcolm X we know and admire today since his assassination in 1965.

Most Black revolutionaries and nationalists start their chronology at the death of Malcolm X, including the Black Panthers. Bobby Seale recalls going to McClymonds High School in Oakland to hear Malcolm X speak and indicated that had Malcolm not been killed, the Black Panther Party probably would not have developed. He would have followed Malcolm in the Organization of Afro-American Unity (OAAU), modeled after the Organization of African Unity (OAU) on the African continent. Malcom X, a.k.a. El-Hajj Malik El Shabazz, would inspire young revolutionaries like Huey P. Newton, Bobby Seale, Eldridge Cleaver, Assata Shakur, Stokely Carmichael, Stokely Carmichael, Timothy Hayes, and many others who yearned to be a free and independent people – by any means necessary.

Analytically, the Black Panthers were much like the Minute Men during America's early colonial period as a group of citizens who stood up to defend the community against the local English colonial power structure. While this is not a perfect analogy as it relates specifically to Black people, it is close enough to draw parallels. Malcolm would use the

White power structure's own history to justify our stand as a people who were by enlarge colonial subjects in the domestic confines of America. He observed that 22 million Black people, at that time, were just as justified to say, "Liberty or death," after 400 years of slavery, hangings, exploitation, and systematic racism in a country that talked democracy but practiced hypocrisy. The Black Panther Party followed Malcolm's example by taking two paragraphs out of the Declaration of Independence of the United States, which was written by colonial subjects of England under the monarchy of King George, III. One paragraph stated, "When in the course of human events, it becomes necessary for one people to separate themselves from the political bands which have connected them to another and to assume amongst the powers of the Earth, the separate and equal stations in which the Laws of Nature and natures God has entitled them, with a descent respect to the opinions of mankind would require that they declare the causes which impel them to this separation."

The 10-point platform and program of the Black Panther Party was Black people's Declaration of Independence or a statement of grievances against the government at that time for social change. Malcolm X had a tremendous impact on the leaders in the Panther movement and would later be granted the distinction as "The Children of Malcolm". When Chicago Black Panther Chairman Fred Hampton was assassinated, along with Panther Mark Clark, there on a blood-soaked bed cover was a book with

Malcolm X's face adorning the cover. Fred was probably reading the book before he went to sleep after being drugged by a police informant named William O'Neal, who had joined the Black Panther Party and elevated to head of Panther security.

Before Bobby Seale met with Huey P. Newton to start the Panther Party, he was preparing to fly out to join the Organization of Afro-American Unity after Malcolm's visit to the Bay Area. However, with Malcolm's assassination, this paved way for his philosophical heirs to come to fruition via the Black Panther Party for Self Defense founded October 15, 1966 in Oakland, California. The Black Panther symbol itself was taken from the Lowndes County Freedom Democratic Party in Alabama as an alternative to both the Republican and Democratic parties since Blacks were denied voting rights in the Deep South. The Self Defense part of their name came from the Deacons for Defense who were deacons in churches that organized to protect civil rights workers and voting efforts in the face of racist aggression. Not one incident of violence occurred when the armed Deacons for Defense were on the scene because they were prepared to speak the language of the Ku Klux Klan, Citizen's Council, local police, or any other opposition if necessary. Malcolm X left the spiritual utopia of the Nation of Islam (NOI) and took a more engaging direct action position that would better affect the lives of everyday Black people outside of the Nation of Islam. Along the way, however, he had met with many revolutionary leaders like Fidel Castro, Che Guevara,

Kwame Nkrumah, and others, which made him believe that revolutionary activism, along with self-defense and self-determination, was the best method to use in our struggle as he began to internationalize our plight- a perspective adopted by the Black Panther Party.

In his "Prospects for Freedom Speech" given in January 1965 he was quoted, "Power in defense of freedom is greater than power on behalf of tyranny and oppression because power, real power, comes from conviction which produces action, uncompromising action." The Black Panther Party understood the need for self-defense and determination; Malcolm said it was our right as human beings. Malcolm stood before the entire world to bring the plight of African Americans before the United Nations, Organization of African Unity, Third World leaders, and others like the Panthers did a few years later. When Malcolm X took part in the famous Oxford Debate in England at the end of 1964, he, like Frederick Douglass a century earlier, condemned western imperialism and colonial domination upon the darker people of the Earth. He did not say it behind doors but right in their faces with no fear. Malcolm was the perfect Black Panther to strike out against oppressors who constantly put Black people's backs against the wall. He was not a stuck up bourgeoisie Negro or reactionary street thug, but a critical thinking, calculated, dedicated revolutionary that would give rise to the Black Panther Party. If we value Malcolm and his wisdom, we need to develop the character for the support of that wisdom because he was truly our Black Manhood. Articulated by Ossie Davis at his eulogy, "He was our manhood, our living Black Manhood." That was his meaning to his people; and in honoring him, we honor the best in ourselves. Long live the spirit of Panther Comrade Malcolm X, our Progenitor Panther, and the Black Panthers who continued his noble mission.

I Am We, But A Bit About Me

In Huey P. Newton's book *Revolutionary Suicide*, Huey eloquently states, "There is an old African saying, 'I am we.' If you met an African in ancient times and asked him who he was, he would reply, 'I am we.' This is revolutionary suicide – I, we, and all of us are the one and the multitude." For me, that is the ultimate goal in discovering your humanity. But before I affirmed we, there was just me. I was born in Miami, Florida on August 24, 1965 to my Louisiana raised parents, James and Vera Robinson, who met at historically Black Southern University in Baton Rouge, Louisiana. My sister Mia Renee Robinson would arrive July 12, 1966, which was 11 months after I was born.

My mother was born in New Orleans but raised in Zackary, just outside Baton Rouge named in French Red Stick. My mother was the eldest of five children born to my grandparents, Jarrot and Rebecca Anderson. My father was from Rayville, Louisiana, which is up in the northern part of the Louisiana. I remember visiting my father's mother, Minnie Perkins, in Monroe a lot. But other than a few relatives there, I didn't know much about Rayville or Monroe, the largest city in northern Louisiana. Mia and I were born in Miami, Florida because my father had gotten a job there. My mother, who had graduated a year earlier, was already working at Capital High School as a teacher and was given an ultimatum to either stay married and go to Miami, or remain in Baton Rouge as a divorcee. Mom obviously chose Miami despite her strong family ties. That made her departure heartbreaking for her, my grandparents and her five other siblings: Mary, Ruby, Barbara, Janice and the youngest, Jarrot, Jr. a.k.a. Mann (Little Man). The Andersons in Zackary were as close as a family could be, including the family across the creek. They were forced to deal with the reality of my mother leaving for life in an unfamiliar city.

I don't remember much about living in Miami since I only lived there the first eight years of my life, but a few things vividly come to mind. One situation was when I was walking home alone from Parkview Elementary in Opa Locka (now Miami Gardens). I was crossing the street when a teenaged girl was yelling at me to come back to the sidewalk after I began to walk across the street. She was frantic, which scared me, so I kept walking when I noticed two Black guys in their late teens or early 20s coming toward me in a car that reminded me later of the car in the Starski and Hutch show. The teenage young lady was now screaming and crying by now, so as a little boy I was very confused until I heard the driver press the brakes and skidding toward me which caused me to freeze. Thank God the car stopped a mere five feet from me and I ran toward my neighborhood looking back at the girl on the sidewalk who had now collapsed on the sidewalk. Being that I came so close to getting hit by a car, I would say that was a very impressionable event that I never shared with anyone until this day. I am glad to be alive to recall it.

I remembered when my friend, Gene who lived across the street, took me and five others for a ride that seemed to last for hours. Upon sunset I return home, my father (who was waiting patiently on our porch), gave me a whipping I will never forget. The Big Wheel gang of five got their ride on but paid a price for it. The other event that left a lifelong impression was when my sister and I were awakened to hear my mother gasping for air after being put in a headlock by my father and my grandmother Minnie attempting to get my father off her. I had witnessed a few events like this before, but I was very young and did not understand what would be called domestic abuse until I was a young adult. I was not a bad kid, but I was always into something or another.

Gene was a natural leader and got all the kids in our neighborhood including me into all sorts of predicaments. Nevertheless, he was a good dude deep down and would later do time in a federal prison for drugs charges. Both of us went to Parkview Elementary, which was very diverse culturally. As such, I found myself crushing on Jamaican, Cuban, and Puerto Rican girls. Years later, I took my wife to my old neighborhood and happened to see Pete, Gene's brother, on the corner with an inquisitive look as I slowed my car to stop. Before getting out the car, I rolled the window down, called his name and told him I was June (which was short for Junior), his next door neighbor. He recognized me and put away the drugs he was prepared to sell to what he thought was a customer. It was great to see my old childhood friends. Finally, Gene came out the house to see his childhood friend. I could tell Gene had a rough life since we had last seen each other as kids, but when we saw each other, it was like being back in the Big Wheel gang Gene organized. Gene took my wife and me back to Parkview. He asked me if I remembered some of the things we would do. I did not remember much of what we did at school, but it still seemed to put a great smile on his face.

After years of abuse, I do remember the day dad was at work when mom left him to return to Louisiana and later divorce him. In the years shortly after, we moved to Cincinnati where my mom's cousin, Emma Dee, lived. I assume now she was trying to avoid my father. She later ended up in Nashville, Tennessee then back to cities in Louisiana like Hammond, Lafayette twice, Tiger Town near Louisiana State University in Baton Rouge (where I would become a very good bike thief), and Lake Charles. My mother was always going to school even though she had a degree from Southern University. She took advantage of the married student housing that housed kids. Even though she was a divorcee, her saving grace was the fact that she had kids. On one of the few times my father was allowed to see my sister Mia and I, he handed me a piece of paper with his phone number on it. I still remember the phone number until this day: 624-2946. I started to let Pops know where we were since I knew he could not do anything to my mother at that point. My father was a smart, intelligent man who I knew loved my sister and me. Because he was abusive to the women in his life, he later married and abused the next wife name Sally. He knew her from his childhood in Rayville. I did not write about this to put my father down, but I believe with counseling or therapy, he could have worked out his issues. Many Black people do not choose to talk to a trained professional or psychologist about their problems. As a result, it grows into what could result in a tragedy. My father and I would later develop a great relationship despite ups and downs to the point of not only being father and son, but friends.

My sister and I went to two high schools, Hammond High in Hammond and Acadiana High in Lafayette, Louisiana. Hammond, Louisiana was the place we stayed the longest time a little over four years. I played football at Hammond Junior High where we were undefeated Parrish Champions. In Louisiana, unlike the rest of the country, we had parishes as opposed to counties, due to the French influence in Louisiana. When my mother moved Mia and me to Lafayette for our final two years of high school, I met my future wife. She was just 14-years old, but she was extremely mature. I always liked Kathy as a friend but was respectful of my friendship with her brother, Joseph, who was my best friend in Lafayette. I first saw Kathy when I visited Joseph at their home. While I was sitting on the porch facing Joseph, he gave me this irritated look while glancing at the glass door behind me. I had to turn around to see what had put such a look on my friend's face. Well, I turned around only to see a pretty young lady absent of any smile. Instead, she had a noticeable frown on her face. Joseph told me she was nice once you got to know her but she was tough and very protective of family, even at that young age of 14. Years later, when Kathy was in college at 21-years old, is when I made my feelings known that I always liked her and that she would make "somebody" a wonderful wife. I was 24-years old at this time and living in Los Angeles, California. This was six years after my mother, Vera, died of pneumonia at the age of 44. My father would die suddenly at 53-years old of an aneurysm nine years later. My mother would always hint at how nice Kathy was. At that time, though, she was not dealing with any boys. Plus, she was too young for me. Mom was right, because we will be celebrating our 22 years of marriage October 29, 2016.

One summer after my junior year at Acadiana High School (where I played football and ran track), I visited my father in Los Angeles. Years earlier, he had moved from Miami, Florida to Cordova, Alaska then to Seattle, Washington. He finally settled in Los Angeles where he had relatives living on the West Coast. My father dabbled in the cocaine drug game in Miami while he was a teacher. I even saw evidence of that while my sister and I visited him there. He later told me that the reason he left Miami was because a hit had been put out on him, so he left and went to the farthest place he could go to stay alive, which was Alaska. I will never know how deep he was in the drug game, but I did notice he had acquired some things like a six-passenger boat and a

Corvette sports car when he lived in Miami but had to sell all these toys when he left Florida. I guess dad was living the life that did not filter down to his children as our mother struggled. I still loved my father no matter what. When my sister and I arrived in Los Angeles for the first time to visit our father, I actually thought downtown Los Angeles was by LAX – Los Angeles International Airport – because of all the big buildings near the airport. I was obviously mistaken. This is not surprising for a country bumpkin like me. Having visited Miami and Houston, the metropolis of Los Angeles was overwhelming as we toured with our father in his little Fiat. As the vibrant young man that I claimed to be, I noticed one clear thing: California had consistent pretty weather and consistent pretty women of all shades, cultures, and nationalities. After a few days there, my little childhood friend Kathy became a distant memory, evaporating like the morning dew. I can say that now and obviously I never forgot about her. Nevertheless, I enjoyed my single days until my late 20s. The city, mountains, beaches, cultures, Hollywood, and cultural diversity were all an eye awakening experience for me. The other "new" experience for me was learning about the Crips and Bloods from my father whose relatives lived in many of those areas in South Central L.A. a.k.a. "The Hood."

My father gave me some words of advice upon my visit about the colors I wore, particularly blue and red. Being a young Black man, he understood my ignorance to the environment he was exposing me to.

Coming from Louisiana at that time, I did not know anything about Black street gangs prior to my visit to Los Angeles until my father's quick gang lecture. Upon my return back home, I remembered the movie "Colors" starring Sean Penn and Robert Duvall giving a stirring depiction of gang life from the perspective of the L.A.P.D. a.k.a. Los Angeles Police Department. Years after that, a movie that touched me even more about street gangs was "South Central." And, of course, "Boyz in the 'Hood" impacted my view of life in South Central Los Angeles. Even as a young teenager, I never understood how brothers could claim a block to defend and kill over, but when the boys in blue a.k.a. cops came; both Crips and Bloods would scatter. Even I was shocked by the inter-gang warfare that would happen within "sets" that would result in death. Certainly, that was a new experience for me.

Another experience that left an impression on me was going to Venice Beach for the first time. This was when I learned that the freaks not only come out at night but also spent their day hanging out at Venice Beach. One of the first things I remember when my father, sister, and I strolled along the boardwalk in Venice was a dude with a guitar, a tall gypsy hat, and a large snake around his neck as he skated up and down the boardwalk. I also saw many break-dancers who were popular during the 70s and 80s, along with street performers, magicians, and musicians. One of my favorite music videos was The Gap Band's "Party Train." It was filmed there along with the movie "Breakin.'" Also, Teena Marie was a blueeyed soul legend from this beach side Haight Ashbury imitation in Southern California called Venice Beach.

It was at Venice Beach when I noticed a shirt some street vendor was selling that had the image of a neatly dressed guy wearing glasses peering out of a window with a rifle in his right hand. Not knowing much about this brother and why he was looking out that window, I instinctively felt it portrayed an image of strength and militancy but would learn that it was a stressful time for him. Later, I read about him being one who was protecting his family after his split with the Most Honorable Elijah Muhammad and The Nation of Islam. His name was Malcolm X. Now it is a painful image to look at because his assassination was one of the most traumatic events in the history of the Black struggle. Yet, it would give birth to the Black revolutionaries to come. Prior to seeing his image on that shirt, I did not know much about Malcolm and how his life would inspire many, so I decided to learn more about him. I read, *The Autobiography of Malcolm X* by Alex Haley. Malcolm influenced many like Muhammad Ali, The Honorable Louis Farrakhan, poet LeRoi Jones a.k.a. Amiri Baraka, poet Sonia Sanchez, musician Gil Scott Heron, Stokely Carmichael a.k.a. Kwame Ture' as well as leading Black Panthers Huey P. Newton, Bobby Seale, Eldridge Cleaver, Assata Shakur, Dhruba Bin Wahad, Herman Ferguson, Fred Hampton, and many others. After reading *The Autobiography of Malcolm X*, I would not only discover a lifelong idol, but the Progenitor Panther who was the inspiration for the Black Panther Party.

The Black Panther Legacy Continued by the New Panther Vanguard Movement _____

The New Panther Vanguard Movement (NPVM), formerly the New African-American Vanguard Movement (NAAVM), was officially launched in Los Angeles, California at the Vision Theater on October 15, 1994 with the "First Annual Remember the Black Panther Party Festival and Forum". The Vanguard was the Panther Party of the 1990s and the new millennium. It was founded by former members of the original Black Panther Party, activists, former members of the Crips and Bloods street gangs, and brothers and sisters in the community who believed it was our individual and collective responsibility to "make the revolution happen". The Vanguard had events like "Remembering the Black Panther Party" festivals, "Serving the People, Body and Soul" programs, Unity in the Community barbeques, Survival Programs as well as Political Education forums held at the New Panther Vanguard Movement International Panther Headquarters in South Central L.A.

These community events included educational speakers, cultural and entertainment activities, networking with other community organizations, tutoring services by college students, and provided services to the homeless. These events had a two-fold objective: (1) to promote the remembrance of the many positive political and social contributions of the original Black Panther Party; and (2) secondly to provide appropriate context for the efforts of the New Panther Vanguard Movement, which was regarded by the original Black Panther Party cadre as the 90s Panther Party. New Panther Vanguard Movement distributed over 20,000 bags of free food to needy families in South Central Los Angeles during their era, along with organizing Survival Programs like the Free Clothes Program, Seniors Against a Fearful Environment (SAFE) program, The Literacy and Computer Instruction program, providing a local doctor to provide basic healthcare to the community via the Community Health Program, and the Busing to Prison program.

The New Panther Vanguard issued the *Black Panther International News Service* in the summer of 1995 which became a national and internationally distributed newspaper. New Panther Vanguard Movement had a 10-Point Platform and Program which became the group's blueprint for change. The New Panther Vanguard Movement dedicated its existence to continuing in the revolutionary spirit of the original Black Panther Party and Malcolm. Brother Malcom X certainly embodied that spirit and put forth a program for the total liberation of Black people, an organization he led, the Organization of African American Unity (OAAU). The Black Panther Party was the first successfully organized attempt to unify the "Liberation Movement" of Black people. New Panther Vanguard Movement understood that the mission had to continue, and since there was no Malcolm X or Organization of African American Unity around now and the Black Panther Party was destroyed by the United States government in its infancy, the New Panther Vanguard Movement stepped forward to fill that void and declared, "All power to the people". The New Panther Vanguard Movement was functional from 1994-200 before disbanding, but left a legacy that Malcom X would have been proud of. It has been recognized by the Black Panther Party members as carrying on in the true tradition of "Serving the People thru Propaganda and Programs". The Black Panther Party members, including cofounder Bobby Seale and It's About Time BPP Committee includes the Vanguard as part of their legacy and participates in Black Panther Party Anniversary reunions.

The Vanguard Movement Continued The Black Panther Party's Great Legacy Of Proper Propaganda: "The Black Panther Newspaper" _____

In 1994, the New Panther Vanguard Movement (formerly the New African-American Vanguard Movement) stepped forward to fill the void left by the Black Panther Party, whose emphasis was to establish a platform designed to serve and liberate the people. Having some former members of the Southern California Chapter of the Black Panther Party in the 70s was important in forming a cadre best equipped to carry this new movement into the 90s, along with younger and new activists who were eager to carry on the noble tradition of revolutionary activism. Propaganda with a Program is Symbol with Substance, so in order to advertise our community programs for the new millennium generation, an effective propaganda tool needed to be created or, in this case, re-created. Hence, *The Black Panther News Service*. Effective propaganda will enable the Black and oppressed community to control its own image and inform the masses to what we want and what we believe as an organizational apparatus to show the people that "our" wants are the same as "theirs."

Just like the Black Panther paper in the 60s and 70s, the community was glad to get our point of view and the paper sold well. Our paper became a steady source of funds to help us develop our programs. The initial quantity printed just 5,000 copies back in the summer of 1996, but it spread like wildfire. The enthusiasm generated because not only a "new Panther" organization emerged for this generation, but also because of what the Black Panther Party's newspaper, *The Black Panther*, meant to the community we were serving as the "Voice of the People". Historically, our community has been constantly bombarded by the negative one sided, reactionary media. This paper provided a communication alternative just like the Panthers in the 60s did for the 90s struggle.

The Black Panther Party was concerned specifically with the basic political aspirations, desires, and social needs of the people and to see that these things were articulated in a "revolutionary fashion," through the effective use of any and all "propaganda tools". Revenue generated from newspaper sales was used to fund community-based "Survival Programs" and organizing activities for the people. The Vanguard Movement understood this concept and adopted this strategy to reach the 90s generation.

To produce the newspaper in the 1990s was a lot easier than in the 1960s because we did not need to use a print-roller press for its mass production. Instead, New Panther Vanguard Movement was able to use modern computer technology with articles saved to disks, format the paper at a local printing company to do the layout, and then have a mass production in a local print warehouse. We would then pick up the bound copies to bring back to headquarters. Each edition of the newspaper would have a volume and number as well as a color code for differentiation.

One of the key decisions we made was not to have a picture of Huey, Bobby, or any person at the head of our organization on the masthead. Instead, we used a picture of a new millennium Panther as the ideological imagine on the newspaper. Using the new Panther image and promoting the community platform took the focus off an individual so we could avoid a cult personality that would define this new effort. We made people pay attention to the principles and guidelines that were related to our platform.

The Black Panther newspaper was our extended Political Education beyond our headquarters that reached beyond the confines of our office in South Central Los Angeles. Also, the newspaper reached people on the national and international level, just like the original Black Panther Party paper. In his autobiography, *Revolutionary Suicide*, Black Panther Party co-founder Huey P. Newton wrote, "In *The Black Panther*, the people read the true explanation of why we went to Sacramento and what happened there. We reported on events and meetings in the Black communities all over the Bay area. Until that time, the Black Panther Party had been maligned by the establishment press that was only interested in sensationalism to sell papers. But once we began to give our own interpretation of events, Black people realized how facts had been twisted by the mass media. They were glad to get our point of view and the paper sold well. Our paper became a steady source of funds to help us develop our programs". The New Panther Vanguard Movement never reached the Black Panther Party's circulation high of 125,000 copies per week, but perhaps with the Internet age, we were able to heighten awareness of what we were about, just like the Panther Party. The Vanguard Movement was honored to carry on the Black Panther Party's tradition of Proper Propaganda.

A View From The Vanguard

After our first annual Remembering the Black Panther Party Forum and Festival at the Marla Gibbs Vision Theatre in Leimert Park section of Los Angeles on October 15, 1994. We had a well attended event full of speeches, tributes, music entertainment, and a free food giveaway of 1,000 bags of free food to needy families. The very next day, October 16, 1994, the first official public meeting of the New African American Vanguard Movement was held at the Elegant Manor on West Adams Boulevard. Kwaku Duren officiated the meeting attended by Shareef Abdullah, Kizzy Brown, Dawood Ingram, Goodie Williams, Hanif Mack, Kwame Welsh, Simba Wa Imani, Sister Sheila, Boko Abar, and others. Our initial meeting was a lot smaller than I expected. I remembered a tall slim elder brother with long gray dreadlocks. He had a very peaceful and regal presence. Later, I learned that he was Ronald Freeman, a former Los Angeles Black Panther who, along with his brother Roland, survived encounters with the Los Angeles Police Department (LAPD) and an infiltrated US Organization in the late 60s. Outside of Ronald Freeman, I was drawn to the three principle former Black Panther Party members who did most of the talking. They were Kwaku, Shareef, and Boko.

Kwaku reorganized the Southern California chapter of
the Los Angeles Black Panther Party from 1976-1981 under the leadership of Elaine Brown who led the Party during that point in its history.

Kwaku was the former Coordinator of the Southern California Chapter of the Black Panther Party. This chapter was reorganized in October 1976 with the support and participation of the Panther leadership in Oakland. Having been released from prison in 1970, by 1972 Kwaku founded and directed the Intercommunal Youth Institute in Long Beach, California, along with other organizers. He became personally involved in issues of police abuse after a California Highway Patrolman killed his sister, Betty Scott, on a highway near Oakland in 1975. At a very young age, Shareef Abdullah was a former member of the reorganized Southern California Chapter of the Black Panther Party under Kwaku's leadership. Shareef was raised in the mean streets of South Central Los Angeles but was indoctrinated into the revolutionary movement very early. Shareef always talked about his memories as a child when he participated in the Party's Free Breakfast for Children program during his school days. Early on, Shareef proved that he was a "Panther" to his heart and was a key figure in growing the Vanguard Movement with his great ability to speak, inspire, and relate to the people.

Boko, who I swear looked like the reincarnation of Ethiopian Emperor Haile Selassie, was a former member of the Black Panther Party with the longest history of all the former Black Panther Party Panthers. He was also a member of the People's Party II (PPII) in Houston, Texas under the leadership of Carl Bernard Hampton, who was assassinated on July 26, 1970 by the Houston Police Department prior to People's Party II finally being granted a Black Panther Party chapter. Boko was an active member of the Queens, New York Black Panther Party as well as working at the National Headquarters of the Black Panther Party in Oakland before relocating to Los Angeles and joining the Black Panther Party chapter Kwaku organized.

Boko was "the Conscious of the Vanguard" and the one I regarded as my mentor during the time we spent together which has resulted in a friendship that lasts today. The rest of the Vanguard Movement was composed of newer activists, both younger and older. They did not have as much experience as the three former Black Panther Party members, but they had all the enthusiasm needed to contribute in an organized struggle. If someone was doing "central casting" for our group compared to the 60s Panthers, Kwaku would be our Bobby Seale, the calm organizer and our chief theoretician; Shareef would be a combination of Huey P. Newton and Bunchy Carter with his ties to South Central L.A. in dealing with brothers on the block, but also an outstanding speaker like Bunchy who commanded respect; I had the Eldridge Cleaver role as the organization's Propagandist with my writing and speaking. I was also chiefly responsible for the initial publication of the re-issued *Black Panther* newspaper; Boko was our Emory Douglas as an outstanding artist but great program organizer; Quadry was our Big Man Howard for obvious reasons (being a big guy) but he had a good speaking voice and was well respected by the young members; and Kamau Osiris in Indianapolis, Indiana later became our Midwest Minister of Defense. He was our version of Fred Hampton with his speaking and organizing abilities. Dedicated brothers like Captain Ron and Larry G., as well as sisters like Kizzy, Goodie, Sister Pat, Sheila, Heidi, and Bridgette, who were a combination of many women from the 60s like a Kathleen, Elaine, Ericka and Akua. Some were in leadership, while others were in the background. But like the sisters in the Black Panther Party, they lead in many of the community programs we offered; the youngsters like Dreamer and Zahkee were our Lil Bobby Hutton and wonderful musical artists and loyal adherents to Shareef's Ministry of Defense.

The original Southern California Black Panther Party chapter, prior to Kwaku's re-organization of this branch in 1976, had been decimated by the murders of many Los Angeles Panthers like Robert Lawrence, Steve Bartholomew, Tommy Lewis, Arthur Morris, Frank Diggs, Nathaniel Clark, and most notably Southern California Black Panther Party leader Alprentice "Bunchy" Carter and John Huggins, who were both murdered at University of California Los Angeles (UCLA) on January 17, 1969 after an incident during a meeting involving alleged members of the cultural nationalist US Organization. Geronimo Pratt, Erika Huggins, Elaine Brown, the Freeman Brothers, Gil Parker, Wayne Pharr, and Mohammed Mubarak were some of the other notable members of that chapter of the Los Angeles Black Panther Party. Incidents around the country like the murders of Fred Hampton and Mark Clark in Chicago, Lil Bobby Hutton in Oakland and countless other attacks and murders of Black Panthers around the country who Federal Bureau Investigations Director J. Edgar Hoover called, "The greatest threat to the internal security of the country," the Los Angeles chapter was the hardest hit of all chapters in the entire Black Panther Party.

With this backdrop of history, the Vanguard Movement, then known as the New African American Vanguard Movement, emerged to the public on October 15, 1994, which was exactly 28 years to the day as the founding of the Black Panther

Party in Oakland by Huey P. Newton and Bobby Seale. Similar to the original Black Panther Party emerging a year after the Watts Riots and the death of Malcolm X in 1965 prior to that, the New Vanguard Movement would emerge after the rebellion resulting from the Rodney King verdict that is popularly called the Los Angeles Riots in 1992. Those events in history would give birth to the domestic revolutionaries of the Black Panther Party and later the revolutionary activists in the New Panther Vanguard Movement who dedicated themselves to carrying on the revolutionary spirit of the Black Panther Party.

The first meeting was essentially a "get to know you" session and applications were taken for review by Kizzy. Also during this particular meeting, Ronald Freeman spoke with the new members about his experience in the Party and the challenges we would face to reach the community during our present era. It was great to hear from someone with experience such as Ronald and he would remain not only a close confidant of the group overall but a wise mentor for me to rely on for advice. Shareef would always proclaim that the Southern California Chapter of the Black Panther Party as the most capable in the entire Black Panther Party. Considering the challenges they faced against the Los Angeles Police Department (L.A.P.D.), Federal Bureau of Investigations (FBI), and various organizations who often worked against the Panthers on a variety of levels. Shareef was right.

Considering the special challenges of being in Los Angeles, it was hard to disagree with Shareef who especially understood the dynamics of South Central Los Angeles, the era of the Bloods and Crips street gangs, and the L.A.P.D. Chief Daryl Gates era in which we were living in at that time. Initially, I was interested in the security cadre that was going to be developed within the Vanguard after seeing so many images of Malcolm X, Minister Farrakhan, and various Black Panther leaders being protected by a phalanx of protectors. Those images were always very powerful, not only because it showed that they had the leaders' well-being in their hands in case of any attempt against them; but also it displayed a powerful image of unity. Simba seemed to be the one who initiated the talk about a security apparatus, so I naturally got to know Simba rather quickly.

While at the Elegant Manor, a free food survival program was initiated, being interviewed by journalist, and developing coalitions other groups. One of the early groups to meet with us was an organization from London, England called Panther. This was a group of Black and East Indian Britons who were very active in the London area and had a well distributed newspaper called *Panther*. After a visit by this group and much dialogue, the Vanguard and the Panther group collaborated on a joint issue of *Panther*, showing our unity in fighting oppression in our respective communities on each side of the Atlantic. Also during that same time, Kwaku visited the Panther group in London and later on, an East

Indian Panther group member, Neelam Sharma, visited Los Angeles from London to film a short 10-minute documentary on our group called "The Vanguard". After a short courtship, Neelam and Kwaku married.

The Vanguard Movement had a number of events where either Kwaku or Shareef gave presentations with me and Simba standing by each speaker looking serious as best we could with our eyes moving slowly, side to side the way I remember the Nation of Islam's Fruit of Islam would look standing next to the Honorable Elijah Muhammad, Malcolm, or Minister Farrakhan. Simba, Kwame and I used to stand post during the Vanguard's early appearances as security. He even stood on stage during a performance of Goodie's band she managed during a Hollywood performance that left a tremendous impression on the audience.

One evening, I found out that the Rap group, Public Enemy, was performing at the House of Blues in Hollywood. I recalled meeting Public Enemy's manager, Malik Farrakhan, in Ghana. Malik was formerly known as actor Tony King who starred in movies like "Sparkle" as Satin Strothers. He also had roles in "Daughters of the Dust," "Black Caesar," "The Toy", and other motion pictures. Malik is the godson of Minister Louis Farrakhan. We went down as a group to meet Public Enemy when Goodie and I spotted Malik standing outside the House of Blues. I walked over and I reintroduced myself to him. He then told us to follow him inside.

Once we all were inside, he escorted us to be seated. He also told us to come backstage in the artist's lounge halfway during the song, "Fight the Power," so we could meet Chuck D., Flavor Flav, and the rest of Public Enemy. The Vanguard caused quite a stir when we went upstairs in full "Panther" wardrobe. Kwaku and I led the group to our table and I recall two young Black women stopping me and Kwaku. They got a good look at our uniforms, badges, and berets. After a quick inspection with amazement on their faces, one of the young ladies said, "Wow! Ok." Kwaku and I smiled then proceeded to our seating area after this spontaneous inspection that was brought about by curiosity.

Interestingly enough, sitting next to us were rap legends Kool Moe Dee and Ice-T; they both gave us approving nods. After enjoying the performance until halfway during "Fight the Power," we made our way backstage to meet Chuck D. and Flavor Flav, who embraced each of us as we stood in the VIP room. Chuck D. was definitely impressed with our group, and I reminded him that we met in Ghana while we attended a conference in 1994. I recalled Public Enemy's performance at Black Star Square Arena in Accra, and he fondly remembered. After the brief introductions, Shareef presented both Chuck D. and Flavor Flav with Vanguard t-shirts and officially drafted Public Enemy into the revolutionary cadre, much to their surprise and appreciation. This was a rare moment to relax and enjoy a night out that did not include our consist work in the community.

Goodie was well connected and would get access to certain houses so that we could organize filling bags of food donated by grocery stores, food banks, and other options we used to serve the community directly. Once we packed the groceries in each bag with the exact content as the others, we would put our organization's flyers in each bag that had our Panther image on the front. Boko was the one who did the artwork for our Panther symbol. He was also a great expert on organizing food giveaways. This process would take hours. After we finished packing the bags, we would go to places like Nickerson Gardens and Jordan Downs where we knew these bags of food would mean the most. In fact, while either en route or in these areas, we often saw many people of all types of ethnicities who looked like they could use some help and offer them free food to survive. Though our focus was the Black community, we knew that poor Whites, Latin, and Asian communities of color needed a hand, too, so we served anyone that looked like they need help. When we passed out the free food, we talked to the people about our programs along with our platform. The New African American Vanguard Movement, as we were known then, had a then eight-point Platform and Program as follows:

Point Number #1:

Peace, Justice, and Reparations

Point Number #2:
Food, Housing, Medical Care, and Education

Point Number #3:
Reform of the United States Criminal Justice System

Point Number #4:
Solving the Drug Problem

Point Number #5:
Sentencing Review and Reductions

Point Number #6:
An End to Police Brutality and Abuse of Power

Point Number #7:
An End to Military Aggression

Point Number #8:
Religious Tolerance and Separation of State and
Religion

Later as the New Panther Vanguard Movement, we
reached a collective compromise with the name
change and expansion of our Platform to 10 points
that went as follows:

Point Number #1:
Peace, Justice, and Reparations

Point Number #2:
Food, Housing, Medical Care, and Quality Education

Point Number #3:
Reform of the United States Criminal Justice System

Point Number #4:
Freedom for All Political Prisoners

Point Number #5:
An End to Police Brutality, Terror, and Abuse of Power

Point Number #6:
Sentencing Review and Reductions

Point Number #7:
 Solving the Drug Problem

Point Number #8: An End to Military Aggression

Point Number #9:
Religious Tolerance and Separation of State and Religion

Point Number #10:
Freedom is All Power to the People

The original Black Panther Party's Platform and Program was as follows:

Point Number #1:
We want freedom. We want the power to determine the destiny of our Black community.

Point Number #2:
We want full employment for our people.

Point Number #3:
We want an end to the robbery by the Capitalists of our Black community.

Point Number #4:
We want decent housing that is fit for the shelter of human beings.

Point Number #5:
We want education for our people that exposes the true nature of this decadent American society. We want education that teaches us our true history and role in present-day society.

Point Number #6:
We want all Black men to be exempt from military service.

Point Number #7:
We want an immediate end to police brutality and murder of Black people.

Point Number #8:

We want freedom for all Black men held in Federal, State, County and City prisons and jails.

Point Number #9:
We want all Black people, when brought to trial, to be tried by a jury of their peer group or people from their Black communities, as defined by the Constitution of the United States.

Point Number #10: We want land, bread, housing, education, clothing, justice and people. And as our major political objective, a United Nations supervised plebiscite to be held throughout the Black colony in which only Black colonial subjects will be allowed to participate, for the purpose of determining the will of Black people as to their national destiny.

Both Bobby Seale and Huey P. Newton cited the influence of the Nation of Islam's newspaper, *Muhammad Speaks*, as one of the main models they used to create *The Black Panther* newspaper. Both 60s and 90s versions of *The Black Panther* newspaper by The Black Panther Party and the Vanguard Movement were, in essence, a list of grievances on behalf of our people in particular and all people in general against the United States government and our Declaration of Independence as colonial subjects within the domestic confines of America.

Since its inception in 1994, The Vanguard Movement had gone through a number of changes in organizational form, including a major change in our "official name" and minor adjustments in our programmatic activities reflexed in our platform. The programmatic goal of the newly named New Panther Vanguard Movement has remained unchanged since the beginning and was evident in our revised Ten Point Platform and Program. Nevertheless, a major change to our organizational structure needed to take place to identify roles in the organization. First formed in 1994, membership was "loosely structured" when individuals had only to fill out a membership form, attend weekly forums, and participate in organizational activities. As a result, even though we had many "members," the necessary high level of dedication and commitment of a member was very low. Many of the members were just satisfied with "looking like" and referring to themselves as "Panthers". The New Panther Vanguard Movement has always had lots of "community supporter" or "event" members who showed up at our large scale events like "Remembering the Black Panther Party, Festivals and Forums", "Unity in the Community Barbeques for the People", and "Free Food Giveaways" when they heard about these events but did little prior to these activities. Later, "actual membership" into the organization was not automatic and only occurred by "invitation". Those of us that started from the inception of the New Panther Vanguard Movement were convinced that we were building a "leadership organization," not looking for "followers". For this reason, membership could only be extended to those who demonstrated serious commitment and dedication to playing a leadership role in building a "revolutionary movement" through practical work, continuous personal development and critical study over an extended period of time.

After many organizational meetings at the Elegant Manor, we started hosting meetings in our homes, apartments, and condos. We decided to host meetings at our homes instead of paying at the Elegant Manor. While hosting a meeting at my apartment, I received a call from Stephanie O'Neal of National Public Radio a.k.a. NPR. She interviewed us for the National Public Radio's Crossroads Program, which also featured Mario Van Peebles, who had recently released a movie about the Black Panther Party called "Panther". The host meetings went on for a while before getting an office that was perfect for both the organization and Kwaku's law practice. It was a shotgun style 2- level building with four apartments upstairs for members. Being our "Chief Theoretician," Kwaku was also a practicing lawyer, which was also beneficial to members, the community and other legal areas for the New Panther Vanguard Movement. We were off and running to serve the people!

International Panther Headquarters
90s Edition_____

On June 24, 1995, we opened our office the "International Panther Headquarters" located at 1470 West Martin Luther King Boulevard in Los Angeles, California. It was an exciting time for our organization in establishing a base of operation in the community we would be serving. The grand opening of our office featured a program for the community wherein we introduced ourselves.

It was important for the community to know that we would provide a place where people could benefit from our various programs, lectures, meetings, events, and other events to fill the needs of the people. For me, it was a feeling of joy mixed with some sadness, due to the fact that one of our original members, Goodie Williams, decided to leave the group over some hurt feelings from the actions of hierarchy resulting in contradictions. (I will delve into that a bit later). After Goodie's departure, I took the initiative to visit her often in between running around the city carrying out various duties. I remember telling her, "I am glad you were an example for me instead me being an example for you". For my own organizational survival, these would be no truer words.

The office was packed with the community, former members of the Southern California chapter of the Black Panther Party like Roland and Ronald

Freeman, Wayne Pharr as well as community activists who came to support our office opening. Much of the credit for acquiring this office goes to Kwaku who was able to get a good deal with this property for his law office and Panther Vanguard Movement space. We hosted a program from 12 noon until 5 p.m. featuring an introduction of the Ministers. They gave brief statements to describe their area of expertise. By that time, I was named Minister of Information in March (a few months earlier) after showing some promise as a speaker, writer, and media contact for the group. I was also elected as the youngest member of the Vanguard's Leadership Council, which was a tremendous honor after showing dedication in my work, tasks, and maturity.

Our other leaders were as follows: Kwaku was our Chairman and Minister of Internal and External Affairs; Boko was Minister of Organizational Affairs; Shareef was our Minister of Defense and Political Education; Dawood Ingram was Minister of Finance; Qadry Suleiman was the Chief of Staff for the Vanguard's Ministry of Defense and staffed the headquarters; and Kizzy was our Secretary General. We also had a host of newer members like Sister Pat, Dreamer Black, Ronald Davis, B.B. Black, Zahkee, Madd Black, Bridgette, Heidi, Chaka Satore', Larry Lewis-Gillett, and Najee Ali of Project Islamic Hope (who I sometimes referred to as "The Hollywood Panther" due to all the pictures I saw of him with celebrities like Halle Berry and others).   Kizzy's son, Keyond, and Boko's son, Chioke, also helped our growth and development as an organization best equipped to continue the community service legacy of the Black Panther Party and Voice of the People.

Interestingly, Dreamer Black, Madd Black, B.B. Black, and others had the moniker of Black at the end of their names were a part of a group of youngsters both talented and committed to the struggle within their own group called Defending All Blacks.   The Defending All Blacks provided the Vanguard with a shot of much needed energy, adrenalin, and enthusiasm.   The Defending All Blacks were integrated within Shareef's Ministry of Defense, the entry point into joining the Vanguard at this point in our history.   I was a fan of conscious Rap which Dreamer and Zahkee were able to reach many youth through their art form at events aside from our community programs at the office or at our political education classes that were on Wednesday nights.

As a group, we had already begun to make an impression in the community with our mobile food giveaways, showing support for other groups, rallies, and other activities without having an office.   Now with a base of operations, we were able to expand our programs with great success.   One of my tasks in the organization as Minister of Information was to help us put out our organization's newspaper and raise the money to do this through a variety of sources.   I remember Boko and I going to Avatar Records to seek financial support as well as plundering my own savings and hitting up some of the "money" people who I knew would offer some support. I felt if we were able to get out the first paper that we would name *The Black Panther*, like the Black Panther Party's newspaper, I knew the next editions of the paper would be possible. One of the proudest moments for me was giving Dawood a check for $2,500, which would finance the cost of 5,000 papers that would be produced for our organization. I remember Dawood calling me personally, when he heard we had the money collected for our first paper.

Some of my duties as Minister of Information included dealing with the media, creating press releases, providing information on our office phone for events, setting up speaking engagements, being a liaison between the Vanguard and other organizations, and, of course, writing and speaking on behalf of the organization. Boko, who had become my mentor at this point, would always ask me, "What did the other Minister of Information do"? I began to study some of the "positive" things that Eldridge Cleaver did for the Black Panther Party and learned a lot. I could never be compared to him because of the time we were living in. Plus, I was very different from him. Even so, many in the community often referred to me as "Young Rage" because of my rally speaking ability. Shareef would always tell me, "Don't be like Eldridge", who he regarded as the one who helped split the Black Panther Party. He had a general disdain for him, but

I thought in some ways I did want to be like him and in other ways, absolutely not. I remember reading *Soul on Ice*, a memoir and collection of essays written by Eldridge Cleaver, which had a profound impact on me as it relates to our perspective as a people psychologically. This was a work reflecting his views developed prior to joining the Black Panthers. I did get to meet Eldridge Cleaver at the Santa Ana Courthouse June 10, 1997, the day Geronimo Pratt was released from prison after 27 years. However, he was pleasant with me as I shook his hand, briefly spoke, and shared a copy of the re-issued *Black Panther* newspaper with him to which he told me, "You know I created this"? I could tell El Rage, as he was called, was a man who went through profound changes in his life. Eldridge Cleaver passed away on May 1, 1998 of a heart attack.

Our required reading at the office focused on books by revolutionary writers like Frantz Fanon's *"Wretched of the Earth"*, *"Soledad Brother"* by George Jackson, Bobby Seale's *"Seize the Time"*, Huey P. Newton's *"Revolutionary Suicide"* and *"To Die for the People"*, *Malcolm X Speaks*, Elaine Brown's *"Taste of Power"*, *"A Long Time Gone"* by William Lee Brent, *"We Charge Genocide"* by William L. Patterson, *Chairman Moa's "Red Book"*, *"The Colonizer and the Colonized"* by Albert Mwmmi, *"The Autobiography of Assata Shakur"*, *"Nine Lives of a Black Panther"* by Wayne Pharr, *"I Write What I Like"* by Steven Biko, *Angela Davis:*

"An Autobiography", along with other books. The purpose for such reading was to develop a global liberation theology in our mindset that would be adapted for our era. We hosted some wonderful community Political Education sessions (later changed to Community Forums) on Wednesdays on a variety of topics. Great speakers from as far away as Nigeria, Europe, Cuba, Mexico, Central America, Asia, and other places to speak to the people at Panther International Headquarters. One of the most popular appearances at our headquarters was

Ramona Africa of the Move Organization in Philadelphia whose leader was John Africa; the most famous supporter of the organization was Mumia Abu Jamal. Ramona was one of the survivors of the 1985 infamous firebombing of the Move residences located on Osage Avenue by the Philadelphia Police Department under the order of then-Mayor Wilson Goode. The bombing killed 11 people inside including founder John Africa, five other members and five children ages 7 to 13. My work schedule changed and I was not able to go to many Wednesday night forums; any free time for me was during the weekday and weekends.

On November 18, 1995, we held the Second Annual Community Forum-Festival "Remembering the Black Panther Party and Million Man March Tribute" at Compton College. This was where The Vanguard Movement, in conjunction with Compton College and our non-profit Community Services Unlimited, would put the event on. The Vanguard was giving away 2,000 bags of free food to needy families at the event. The secondary theme of our event was recognizing the Million Man March that took place a month earlier in Washington, D.C., which drew many Black men after the call from the Honorable Minister Louis Farrakhan to come to the nation's capital for a "Day of Atonement". Even though marching was not the "Panther way", we were more programmatic than platformatic a.k.a. theory to practice, the March was still supported by the Vanguard Movement.

Several intense meetings at Compton College resulted in a well-planned event. The Nation of Islam hosted an event two weeks prior to our event at the college where I spoke to advertise our event. Tony Muhammad, Western Regional Minister for the Honorable Louis Farrakhan, hosted this event. I spoke with him about our upcoming event. He was already aware of it and promised that there was no way he could not be there to speak. As we prepared for the Compton College event, there was still no other word from Tony Muhammad or any other representative of the Nation of Islam the week of the event. However, we still kept organizing and making media
appearances to advertise the event. This included me and another member named Chaka Satori as guests on the popular KJLH, a radio station owned by music legend Stevie Wonder. On the radio, we told the listeners about the event and the program to take place, including music and speakers. The day of the

event, we saw a few "new" volunteers we had not seen before including a young man of East Indian ethnicity. He was very enthusiastic about helping, but we noticed he had a very observing and suspicious nature about him. Shareef pulled me aside and told me to keep him close and if he was, indeed, a "pig", he would be a "Serving the People" pig today. This meant I had him ride with me to the event. He talked a lot in the vehicle, but once we arrived at the venue, he just looked around like he was taking mental notes. I figured he was a "pig" but I made sure he was going to "work" that day, so I had him set up chairs and hang banners with me. After about an hour, he told me he was going to the bathroom. I never saw him again to this day. At least this pig contributed to "Serving the People" for an hour and a half.

The Second Annual Community Forum-Festival was a very successful event with a variety of musicians, speakers, libation blessings, and reiteration of the legacy of the Black Panther Party and Million Man March acknowledgement. Groups like the Watts Prophets, WaDaDa, Aztlan Mexica Nation, Defending All Blacks, Allah's Army, and other musical entertainers were all well received by the crowd. Speakers included Vanguard leaders, US Organization representatives (who I had approached after the Nation of Islam's event two weeks earlier) came through and spoke to the people. In the late 60s, the US Organization and the Los Angeles Black Panther Party had a well-documented history. As such, I always said, "We cannot carry past pains in our present struggle", which I was quoted in the *Los Angeles Watts Times* after speaking at a Kwanzaa event held at US Organization headquarters. Conspicuously absent was the Nation of Islam and Tony Muhammad. There was not even an assistant minister to speak at the event.

After the event, we met (the next day on Sunday) at our headquarters and discussed the Nation of Islam's absence and how it would be addressed. Shareef was not happy about the actions of the Nation and I spoke with him about the positive dialogue I had with them two weeks prior to our event. He told me that he and the Vanguard's Ministry of Defense would "handle it" that week. Shareef and the "brothers" went down to Mosque #27 that very week. As legend goes, "Those who know won't say, and those that will say really don't know" is what happened in terms of what went down at the temple. After a visit from the Vanguard's Ministry of Defense that day, I received a frantic call from Tony Muhammad who told me that there must have been a misunderstanding. He said, "We want peace between our organizations". I was not surprised in his apologetic tone. Afterward, Tony Muhammad and the Nation would appear at any event we put on and vice versa. Tony Muhammad was a good brother but Shareef wanted to make the Nation "accountable". I was just glad that we could move on.   With our programs and events, we kept busy at Panther International Headquarters.

Serving The People Programs And Coalitions_____

Early on, I realized that a platform without a program is symbol without substance, so I was fortunate to be a part of an organization that took the creed of the Black Panther Party to carry theory into practice. Huey P. Newton was quoted as saying, "There will be those that will only want to be known in the media, but we best judge ourselves by establishing community survival programs". In the 90s, there were groups who claimed the imagery of the Black Panther Party to get the media's attention without one program for the people. With the guidance of former members of the Los Angeles Black Panther Party, we in the Vanguard had the focus to serve our community and build coalitions across racial boundaries. Race has always been very much a part of America's one sided capitalistic social order.

Nevertheless, it is not the ultimate issue to our group because, at the end of the day, it's about the people. Cooperational humanism did not allow our organization to criticize solely based upon race because on a humanitarian level it was not a good thing to do. While our focus was the Black community, we allowed for non-racial coalitions on a variety of issues. Eldridge Cleaver used to say that is was important for the Black Panther Party to build "specific coalitions for specific purposes" to get things done collectively on areas of agreement. Politics historically has shown that there are no permanent friends or enemies, only permanent interests.

Outside of the free food giveaways, we also acquired a bus which we used for our Busing to Prisons Program. We parked the bus in the rear of our headquarters. Quadry would usually be the driver and mechanic to make sure the bus made its Saturday morning run to a nearby prison, transporting family members and some Vanguard members to sell our newspaper at these facilities. Family members would ride for free and only donate on their own without being asked because that was our service to the community.

The SAFE program was a program modeled after the Black Panther Party with members escorting elders either to cash a check, grocery shopping, or any other necessities we could help with if they signed up for our program. Martyred Los Angeles Black Panther Party leader Bunchy Carter's mother, Nora Carter, was a volunteer at the South Central Senior Center off Manchester Avenue where I would go sign up seniors for our Seniors Against Fearful Environments (SAFE) program. With the new electronic payment age, some elders did not need to go to check cashing places but we would get other duties assigned to assist our elder community.

Other programs, like the Computer Literacy Program, introduced youth and adults to the "new" computer phenomena in the 90s emerging technological age. Some of the 60s members of the Party used to tell me about how they had to work with the print media press process for newspapers or rollers back in their day. Now they saw how easy it was to put the information on a computer disk and get the articles "laid out" in digital format. I remember my father being involved in printing for the school he taught at and how you had to be able to read backwards. The new computer technology age was very valuable to our generation and that is why we had computer classes at headquarters for adults or kids who wanted to learn. Certain nights during the week anyone could stop by or if an appointment was made, they would get individual instruction on the basic use of computers.

The Vanguard would organize donations of clothes by making sure donated items got washed, ironed, and folded in size-appropriate containers for either the homeless or needy families requesting such items as clothes or shoes. On many occasions, I would get a knock on the front door of our headquarters by the homeless or people who knew we could help with basic necessities. I would make them size-appropriate clothes container and whatever else they needed. In the office, we kept boxes of non-perishable items to give away, and recommended some referral programs if additional assistance was needed. We would get donations of canned food. Some of the businesses that we talked to about community donations would give non-perishable food or day old bread that we could immediately give the people. This program was in addition to the large food giveaways we would have for thousands of people.

The Vanguard had a WIC program (Women, Infants and Children Program) in our office to help mothers with nutrition for their children. Many mothers in the community signed up for this at the New Panther Vanguard Movement Headquarters. Once a week at Panther International Head Quarters, a local Black doctor named Dr. Phillip Johnson would donate his time by providing free healthcare screenings at the Vanguard office for anyone who stopped by, or if appointments were made by our office staff on Saturdays from 9 a.m. until 12 noon when the physician would come to see people. Healthcare has always been a major issue in the Black and poor community and part of our platform addressed the need for providing this much-needed service to the people. The Vanguard provided a clean area in the middle part of our office for the physician and a sitting area near this room for clients or families. Another very important program held at the Vanguard's International Panther Headquarters was a Free Beast Cancer educational seminar hosted by Breast Cancer survivor Gloria Harmon.

Dialectical Materialism was the ideological philosophy of the Black Panther Party in instituting programs for the community using concrete analysis of concrete conditions that can lead to the Black community's survival and political development. The original vision of the Party was the development of programs for the people as an essential lifeline for the community they were serving. During the 90s, the Panther Vanguard Movement understood this when it emerged in 1994. A program of practical application, as Huey P. Newton outlined in *To Die for the People*, would be the "model" for the community to follow and appreciate. A beneficial program was important to the community for its survival and we were happy to provide those services. The New Panther Vanguard Movement not only understood these ideas but put forward programs for the people in our era as a "primary" tool for recruitment and serving their needs. Had the New Panther Vanguard Movement presented the para-military front from the start, it would have been detrimental to not only the people but also the programs and our organizational survival would be threatened considering the disruptive, murderous tactics this government used against "revolutionary nationalist" organizations like the Black Panther Party.

Huey P. Newton's quote in his book, *To Die for the People*, eloquently stated the community objectives of the Party: "When Bobby Seale and I came together to launch the Black Panther Party, we had observed many groups. Most of them were so dedicated to rhetoric and artistic rituals that they had withdrawn from living in the twentieth century. Sometimes their analyses were beautiful, but they had no practical programs that would translate these understandings to the people. When they did try to develop practical programs, they often failed because they lacked a systematic ideology which would help them make concrete analyses of concrete conditions and gain a full understanding of the community and its needs".

The Panther Vanguard established many coalitions across the board from very diverse organizations like The Exodus organization, The Nation of Islam, the Brotherhood Crusade, the Malcolm X Grassroots Organization, the Brown Berets, American Indian Movement, National People's Campaign, Jay and the Resist and Exist Anarchists, Coalition Against Police Abuse with Michael Zinzun, Congress of Racial Equality (CORE), Dorothy Height's National Council of Negro Women, student groups and many other organizations, including the Free Fred Hampton, Jr. campaign after the son of Fred Hampton was railroaded to prison on a false charge of doing damage to a Korean liquor store during the aftermath of the Rodney King verdict. The campaign was spearheaded by his mother, Akua Njeri, who headed the African People's Socialist Party's National People's Democratic Uhuru Movement (NPDUM). I would fly out from Los Angeles (and later from Atlanta once I made my move there) to not only work with Akua, Kamau Osiris, and NPDUM in Chicago and also visit Fred, Jr. while he was in prison accompanied by Kamau. Our newspaper, *The Black Panther*, published many articles from Fred Hampton, Jr. as well as had features on Akua and National People Democratic Uhuru Movement.

One of the more controversial coalitions we made was with the US Organization who had a history of violence with the Black Panther Party in the late 60s and early 70s. Having known many comrades from the Los Angeles Chapter of the Black Panther Party under the leadership of Alprentice "Bunchy" Carter, I was well aware of those past contradictions between the two groups orchestrated by the local police, government officials, and possible organizational envy or jealousy that resulted in the assassination of Bunchy Carter and John Huggins. A few Los Angeles "Panther Vets" and Former New York Black Panther Safiya Burkari were against our dealing with the US organization. Ronald Freeman was always very positive when I spoke with him about The US Organization despite his experience with this group and how the younger generation of their membership should not be accountable for the burden of the past. I understood that in our era, we cannot carry past pains in our present struggle for collective advancement.

I first encountered US Organization members at a meeting hosted by Compton College, co-host of our Second Annual Remembering the Black Panther Party Festival Forum and Million Man March tribute a few weeks from the meeting. A week later, we hosted a support function for the event at Compton College where I spoke on behalf of the Vanguard. I introduced myself to Subira Kifano who was the US Vice Chair and Organizer. Subira was very kind. He was a few years older than me, but he would have been too young during the tumultuous era between US and the Panthers. After I left the event, I went to our headquarters and spoke with Kwaku who actually had been on panels with Maulana Karenga, head of the US Organization, founder of Kwanzaa and the subject of much suspicion. Formerly known as Ron Everett, Maulana Karenga had a much publicized past not unlike a few of the leading members of the Black Panther Party (such as Eldridge Cleaver, who served time as a rapist prior to joining the Party). I did not particularly care for Karenga because of his past, but there were many young members of his organization that were visible in the community who I felt we could work well with us. Also, I liked the concept of Kwanzaa, which was a way Black people could recognize our culture through celebration. Being somewhat of a cultural nationalist, I caught some flak amongst a few first generation comrades. However, I understood their perspective that the only culture relevant to our community was a people's revolutionary culture.

Establishing these various coalitions took our Chairman Kwaku to places like London where he established a working coalition with groups there, and I have traveled as an emissary for the Panther Vanguard to Johannesburg and Cape Town, South Africa to meet with members of the Pan Africanist Congress like PAC Secretary General Khoisan X a.k.a. Bennie Alexander. I also met with Elizabeth Sibeko, Pan African Congress member, and widow of assassinated Pan African Congress leader David Sibeko, along with Elizabeth's son, Bongani Sibeko (a member of the Pan Africanist Congress whom I met in Johannesburg and later traveled with him to

Cape Town). My previous trip to Africa had facilitated some of these connections thanks to the Nation of Islam's International Representative Akbar Muhammad who I traveled twice with his Adventures in Africa Tours. He was always great at bringing African - African American groups together. I have always respected Akbar's role in the Nation and tried to do that for the New Panther Vanguard in building international coalitions.

The Black Panther Collective (BPC) in New York City, like the New Panther Vanguard Movement, had former members of the Black Panther Party in its leadership and began instituting programs in the New York City area, especially the police surveillance and recording that is now the rage. The Black Panther Collective was organized in 1994 which was the same year of the emergence of the Panther Vanguard. The Black Panther Collective had a 4-part organizational objective: (1) to continue the revolutionary legacy of the Black Panther Party; (2) to put forth a vision of a new and just society; (3) to build a revolutionary infrastructure; and (4) to engage in protracted revolutionary struggle. In early 1998, the Black Panther Collective expanded its police-monitoring program by creating its Brutality Prevention Project whose objective was to mobilize the communities of Blacks, Latinos, and the poor to be active participants in the operation and development of community controlled police observation teams. The Brutality Prevention Project was an effort to expose corruption and misconduct of the police and to insure fair treatment by the police.

This project was conducted in the spirit of the original police patrols of the Black Panther Party organized by Huey P. Newton and Bobby Seale. The Black Panther Collective inspired the Black and Latino communities in Harlem, Washington Heights, and other sections of New York City to obtain the financial, educational, and political resources to operate their own Brutality Prevention Projects in these areas.

In October 1998, a National Panther Summit between the New Panther Vanguard and the Black Panther Collective, along with an unexpected guest named Khalid Abdul Muhammad of the New Black Panther Party and other "invitees" met in a Harlem office near the world famous Apollo Theatre. The Summit consisted of two parts: a public forum that was open to anyone and a closed session attended by representatives from various Panther formations. The closed session involved discussions on ideology, platform, and program of the "new" Panther formations. The Summit dialogue produced some extended discussions and heated debate about the differences between the Dallas-based New Black Panther Party and formations like The Panther Vanguard and Black Panther Collective. These groups together were critical of the open display of guns at public meetings by the New Black Panther Party. They met with us at an event in Houston for Boko's comrade Carl B. Hampton tribute and at a Panther Summit in Los Angeles which the New Black Panther Party founder Aaron Michaels attended. The critical coverage of the New Black Panther Party in the Vanguard's newspaper, the re-issued *Black Panther* newspaper, was also the subject of a heated debate with Khalid Abdul Muhammad who aligned with the New Black Panther Party as National Spokesman.

Despite the initial intense atmosphere on the subject of the New Black Panther Party, several encouraging developments took place: (1) a commitment to move forward on the adoption of a unified 10 Point Platform and Program; (2) the development of standardized membership criteria and a Code of Conduct; and (3) the continued support for a National Outreach Committee responsible for implementing decisions made and reaching out to and communicating with other Panther formations or interested individuals including attempting to offer guidance to the New Black Panther Party (which became obvious that they were going in another direction after Khalid was in the organization). I developed a personal friendship with Brother Khalid, but the direction of the newly influenced New Black Panther Party, including Khalid's understudy Malik Zulu Shabazz, caused the New
Panther Vanguard Movement and Black Panther Collective to let them do "their thing". We did remain open to any counsel if asked, but that never happened.

Some of these issues discussed at these types of summits are best not reported since they involved "critical" opinions on which agreement could not be reached but were necessary in the various stages of the process of building a new National Panther Movement. As such, it gave all of us the opportunity for principled discussions to move forward. In New York, we were so impressed with the members of the Black Panther Collective like Geoff, Kwame from New Jersey and the wonderful sisters in the Collective. Similar to the New Panther Vanguard, after 10 to 12 years of operation, the Black Panther Collective disbanded for a variety of reasons, but left an impact in New York City and distinguished themselves as continuing the great legacy of the Black Panther Party whose first generation Alum count as part of the "Panther history" in New York.

On July 26, 1997, the New Panther Vanguard Movement spearheaded an event with the Houston Black United Front and the S.H.A.P.E. Community Center for a tribute program to Carl Bernard Hampton, a 21-year old leader of People Party II, which later became the Houston Black Panther Party. Carl was assassinated by the Houston Police Department on July 26, 1970. Boko was Carl's close comrade and was there the night Carl was murdered. During Carl's time in Houston, the Black Panther Party was not allowing additional chapters so People's Party II was organized and led by Carl B. Hampton; Boko was a member of this organization. Carl was a powerful speaker and organizer in the Houston community who knew that Black people would remain powerless unless they organized themselves to demand changes in their community.

The day Carl was assassinated by the Houston Police Department (HPD), the Houston Police used the roof of a Black Baptist church at the approval of the pastor to set up a sharpshooter that killed Carl Hampton that evening during a police "sweep" of the neighborhood. Boko had planned an event in tribute to Carl B. Hampton for years, which came into reality. The coalitions that took part in this historic event made it a highly successful program, which included distributing 500 bags of free food for the needy in the community. Carl was only 21-years old when he was murdered, like Fred Hampton in Chicago. Despite his youthful age, it became clear that he was dedicated to his people. Shortly before his assassination, Carl was quoted as saying, "We need revolution and revolution is not necessarily a violent confrontation. If the Black community would organize, we would become a powerful people". This was one of our best coalitions, but some coalitions are more difficult than others when it comes to collectively developing something tangible for the people.

The Hair and Nail Shop Revolutionaries _____

A Hair and Nail Shop Revolutionary is a person or group who has created an emporium that deals in the superficial or external beauty with a focus on image and platform over programs that impact the community. These types of people or groups are interested in building a presence in the media instead of the community. After hearing about a group in Dallas, Texas that emerged in 1989 and organized by a Dallas radio show assistant named Aaron Michaels, a few years prior to the 1994 introduction of the Vanguard Movement, I was among the "leading members" of the Vanguard to travel to Texas to meet the New Black Panther Party along with Milwaukee-based Black Panther Militia member, Kamau Osiris (who was from Indianapolis, Indiana). Kamau joined the Vanguard Movement a year later as our Midwest Panther Vanguard representative. Our groups would meet in Dallas to discuss the possibility of creating a "national Panther organizational structure" involving the New African American Vanguard Movement, as we were known then, along with the New Black Panther Party and any "Panther" representatives that emerged across the United States during that time. My comrade and mentor, Boko, and I had traveled together from Los Angeles to Houston two days prior to going to Dallas via car rental. Boko stayed with his mother and I stayed with an uncle of mine on my father's side. During the Houston stay, I really enjoyed meeting Boko's relatives and seeing some of the places and neighborhoods he grew up in as a youngster. Houston is a "Bayou City" like those I knew from living in Louisiana, so I remember him telling me about crawfishing in one of the many ditches around Houston and also describing that Texas heat while doing it. As a person growing up in humid environments like Texas and Louisiana, a handy sweat rag was a necessity which accompanied most young brothers there.

When our stay in Houston ended, Boko and I headed up to Dallas for the December 20, 1996 meeting with the New Black Panther Party and others. On the way, I realized there it had been a long time since I had visited Texas. My first time in Dallas I was surprised how cold it would get there between 30- to 40degree temperatures. We did a lot of talking on the way until we arrived at this Baptist church in a Black area in the Dallas suburbs where the meeting would take place. Another contingent of Vanguard members were already there waiting in a van, and we proceeded together inside the church to the upstairs meeting room. There were members of the New Black Panther Party including founder Aaron Michaels. Second in command was Robert Williams. Aaron "chaired" the meeting but got off to somewhat of a slow start before Kwaku interceded and requested a meeting structure that would make the meeting more fluid and formatted so that the dialogue would have greater purpose instead of just talking or "chopping it up". Aaron agreed and we commenced to an organized agenda along with collateral points based upon the differences between our groups and how we could be cohesive in building something tangible for a national Panther organized movement.

After about two hours of discussion, we reached a tentative agreement on several points, including the formation of a "National Black Panther Outreach Committee" composed of representatives from each of the groups assembled. This committee had the task of continuing to discuss and reach agreement on issues like "local autonomy," a common agenda or common platform and program, a "Black Panther Code of Conduct" and organizing a follow-up meeting or conference involving all concerned Panther groups from across the country.

The Dallas meeting was hampered by the absence of other representatives of the Black Panther Militia, with the exception of Kamau Osiris and Khalid Abdul Muhammad who began to be associated with the Dallas New Black Panther Party along with other groups. From the beginning of the Vanguard Movement's emergence in October 1994, we had been committed to developing "operational unity" and with cooperation between all community based organizations that were dedicated to the political and economic empowerment of Africans in America. The Vanguard was particularly committed to stirring the revolutionary "Black Panther" sentiments that existed amongst all oppressed peoples and communities domestically and internationally.

Our follow-up meeting would take place during the spring of 1997 in Los Angeles at our headquarters, Panther International, located at 1470 West Martin Luther King Jr. Blvd. in South Central Los Angeles. Only Aaron Michaels came representing the New Black Panther Party and Kamau Osiris attended as the New Panther Vanguard's Midwest representative (having left the Black Panther Militia). Kamau had been staying with me and my wife a day before Aaron was scheduled to arrive in Los Angeles. The next day Aaron arrived and called me about any hotels I knew about near the office, so I offered for him to stay at our apartment since no arrangements had been made for his accommodations. Kamau and Aaron slept in our front room and later we enjoyed some of my wife's Louisiana style cooking. No organizational coordination was made to contact Aaron about accommodations by our hierarchy, so I felt I had to step up and ease his worries. He seemed to enjoy our apartment in Carson, California across from the mall, and he had known Kamau for years so he was very relaxed. I found Aaron was very intelligent and well spoken on my second time being around him but I had a feeling this was a "courtesy" trip in our dialogues at the apartment.

The Summit at the headquarters would take place the second day after Aaron arrived, so I was able to take both Kamau and Aaron to some places of interest around Los Angeles. Aaron indicated that he really liked Los Angeles for his first trip out there and had he been younger, it may have been a good place to live. The day of the Summit we headed to the Vanguard headquarters for the internal meeting. I must admit I was excited about Aaron seeing how we served the people and had a direct relationship with the community. Within the New Panther Vanguard Movement, we were serving in the true spirit and tradition of the Black Panther Party. After the internal meetings at the Summit, I noticed what I would learn later was a Dutch filming crew.

They were filming some of our open sessions which would later be turned into a Dutch language documentary featuring former Dallas Black Panther Party member Fred Bell, Aaron Michaels of the New Black Panther Party, and the Panther Vanguard Movement. The documentary seemed to spotlight the difference between the New Black Panther Party and former Panthers like Fred Bell. The Vanguard did not have a part in this conflict but was featured with autonomy.

While Aaron did show interest during the Summit, I could feel that his mind had been made up regarding the political direction of the New Black Panther Party and Khalid Abdul Muhammad and certainly history would bear this out very soon after our event. The theoretical differences between the New Black Panther Party and the New Panther Vanguard Movement were too vast from our programmatic community service, Black Panther Party themed revolutionary activism approach against the ever increasing Black Nationalist armed media focused approach. I truly believed when we invited the New Black Panther Party to Houston Texas for the event in tribute to Carl Hampton, they would be inspired to get involved in the community via programs. But even then, Quanell X (formerly of the Nation of Islam) was there with the New Black Panther Party, albeit sitting in a limousine until he was scheduled to speak on stage during the event.

At the Houston event, we gave away 500 bags of free food to needy families. Members of the New Black Panther Party seemed to really enjoy serving the people, but that hope was short lived. At one point during the LA Summit, Aaron motioned for me and Kamau to go outside which caused some confusion from Kwaku and Shareef on why Aaron was leaving. He was asked to return for the conclusion, which he did. Afterwards, we returned back to me and Kathy's apartment. I knew Aaron was going to stay a day and a half more, so I took Aaron over to Kwaku and his new wife, Neelam Sharma, to stay with them to get to know Kwaku a little more. I hoped this would influence him to go the substance program route rather than the Platform symbolic position. Both Aaron and Kamau left to go back to their respective homes in Dallas and Indianapolis.

After the Los Angeles Summit, Shareef and Kwaku wanted to speak with me about what happened with Aaron and his abrupt desire to leave during one of the closing sessions. This caused some confusion based upon Aaron's lack of enthusiasm at the Summit. I felt both of them thought that somehow I had something to do with his behavior, but nothing could be further from the truth. I honestly felt he was not interested in any guidance from our cadre or following our direction programmatically.

Like my comrades in the Vanguard, I was hoping he would expand his own program beyond the gun displays and press conferences, but I think with the national standing of Khalid Muhammad, which brought more media, and a more Khalid inspired Black Nationalist theory would be the way Aaron and the New Black Panther Party would go. We in the Vanguard considered ourselves Revolutionary activists or as some considered us in the tradition of Black Panther members, Revolutionary Nationalists.

Aaron, along with Robert Williams, had their reasons why they decided not to work with us in a post by Dhoruba Bin-Wahad. As time went on, though, we decided to disassociate them from the new direction of the New Black Panther Party.

Statements by Dhoruba Bin Wahad, Robert Williams, Aaron Michaels on the "New" New Black Panther Party infused with former Nation of Islam members, most notably Khalid Abdul Muhammad, Malik Zulu Shabazz, and others:

Dhoruba Bin Wahad: Operation Shutdown and Drawing Political Lines on IMIXWHATILIKE dated 7/13/2015 one month prior to Dhoruba and others being assaulted on August 8, 2015 in Atlanta,

Georgia during a New Black Panther Party Conference which had nothing to do with former New Black Panther Party members Aaron Michaels, Robert Williams, and other former members of that original cadre.

Dhoruba Bin Wahad:

After receiving a flyer promoting a New Black Panther Party "round table" to be conducted in Early August, in Atlanta, I, in consultation with comrades across the country, believe that the present conditions demand a full disclosure of both the origins of the New Black Panther Party and the role they play and have played as an encapsulated organization of the racist Right and how that's used by Rightwing agendas to demonize all perceptions of Black revolutionary traditions and historical legacy of organizations such as the original Black Panther Party. While it is of little concern how racists misrepresent legitimate people's movements and revolutionary leaders, when this misrepresentation is a matter of encapsulation, misdirecting, and confusing both activists and non-activists who are sincere, it's paramount that the truth is laid bare for all to see. This is one of those times. With a young generation of activists on the front lines who think the New Black Panther Party has some history or continuation with the original Black Panther Party, and therefore enjoy credibility from this misperception – the time is now to set the records straight.

Too many older activists have gone along with New Black Panther Party charades as a revolutionary Black Nationalist Pan-African formation on the one hand and Black community self-defense force on the other. They have collaborated with them on a number of events, programs, and Black Power displays that have resulted in absolutely nothing concrete or enduring other than to boost the egos of their professed leaders. Undoubtedly, some will decry my actions now and characterize me as a "hater" or an envious little old man as one of the New Black Panther Party leaders said when I and others attempted to persuade them to actually grow some "political analysis other than "hate Whitey" and initiate concrete survival programs and support Political Prisoners, none of whom, by the way, endorse the New Black Panther Party and its arrogant posturing leadership.

Recently I wrote about the "stealth history" of revisionism. I pointed out that distorting the legacy of Black radical traditions was a real strategy of The Counter Intelligence Program or popularly known as COINTELPRO aimed at disconnecting the struggles of one generation from the other. When I responded to the Charleston NAN, initial misrepresentation of the original Black Panther Party as the equivalent of the KKK. NAN responded with an apology for the confusion, and their leaders then went on to lambast the New Black Panther Party and their leaders for using the same tone as racist government and rightwing media. However, the routine opportunism the New Black Panther Party has displayed ever since it was hijacked from Texas community activists in the early 90s by disgruntled Nation of Islam followers of Khalid Muhammad should not continue to go unchecked. Neither the history of the initial New Black Panther Party or the current disarrayed formation with that same acronym had anything to do with the historical Black Panther Party / Black Liberation Army or their ideological orientation. Finally, on the posted flyer are a few individuals whose political commitments and practice are genuine.

But one, Fred Hampton, Jr., the son of my slain comrade, had his name placed on this flyer without his knowledge. This tactic is typical of the New Black Panther Party whenever it wants to grab public attention from a controversy or thrust themselves in the forefront of "the movement". It is for this reason I think the time is right to draw clear lines of demarcation between the detractors from the liberation process and contributors. Like the Black comprador class whose role in controlling Black rage and mis-leadership are becoming common knowledge, groups like the New Black Panther Party and its cultish narrow nationalism must also become common knowledge. Social Practice is the criteria for truth here. Using that gauge, read the following from the original founder of the New Black Panther Party, Aaron Michaels. It was dated in 2013 when the old Black Panther Party members clashed with

New Black Panther Party leadership around the fiasco of the "Million Youth March for Trayvon Martin" and in commemoration of the anniversary of the first "Million Youth March" called by Khalid Muhammad when only a handful of people actually attended despite a loaded speakers list (most of whom also never showed up after initial "endorsement"). It is no coincidence that, once more, the New Black Panther Party leaders are faking another Summit in anticipation of Black August, Attica Rebellion Memorialization, and a repeat of the Million Man March scheduled for October. I should remind everyone reading this extensive post to be mindful that without principled unity, there is no unity at all.

To: Dhoruba Bin

PEACE...

Brother Dhoruba, it has come to my attention that there are a number of issues that have been long standing in regards to the New Black Panther Party and its origins, as well as who is supposed to be in charge of the organization to date.

First, to all the brothers and sisters who have been involved with the organization that I created, and continued to try either in part or whole in making it an organization of principles and not "personalities" I salute you all. I must also add my discontent with the two mendacious individuals who have claimed the leadership of the organization without first of all talking with me first.

This letter is being written in hopes that anyone who reads it will get a better understanding and appreciative vantage point of all the sacrifice that had gone into re-creating the basic ideas of the founding beliefs of the voter registration movement which promoted the voter registration organization known as Black Panther Party from Lowndes County, Alabama and attributed to the idealistic formation of the Oakland, California group known as the Black Panther Party for Self-Defense.

There are many tactical points that will be added to this lengthy letter so that whomever reads it can at least follow the historical points and true history of this organization, and not "believe the hype" and nonsense of "Tweedle Dee-and Tweedle Dumber" (b.k.a. "The Ass-Holes from Down Under.")

First of all, the New Black Panther Party was created in Dallas, Texas in October of 1987 after much research and contemplation. Two and a half years later, I met Dhoruba Bin Wahad (a formerly incarcerated political prisoner) who became a comrade and special consultant of mine, and even greater ally of the New Black Panther Party.

His unusual insight and first- hand experience with the COINTELPRO Program as well as the cruelties of the American legal system, law enforcement and the FBI opened the continued conversation for the need of an organization such as the New Black Panther Party; and in the continued political climate that all people and especially African Americans were continuing to live in America.

I am going to add another point of view to this letter besides my own; an individual who continued to stay in the NBPP after I decided to diminish my role and leave the organization to keep confusion from being the growth of the organization, Robert Williams took the task of being the Chairperson of the NBPP in Dallas and then a nation position before Malik and Hashim even became members of this group.

One of the problems this organization has is people who have joined it "want to be revolutionaries" but have no military experience at all, which is part of the holistic problems and issues that continue to plague the NBPP to date.

I will add Robert Williams' info into this letter as historical record for those who were around at the time of the inception of the NBPP and continue to try to meander thru this group, and working in dim light.

From this point forward, I will allow Robert Williams to give you some of the historical evidence that has taken place over the years; some of those issues allowed Khalid Muhammad to be invited to join the NBPP ranks and, thereby, become the National Chairman of the NBPP...

Robert Williams Historical Perspective below has been added to this document to make sure you follow the truth, and not lies that are being perpetuated by the "So Called Leadership" of the NBPP...

"It was at one of these school board meetings that I was exposed to the impact the NBPP truly had. During one of the meetings, the school board members tried to stop a parent from continuing to voice concerns after the 3- minute buzzer went off. The NBPP had enough of the community from being silenced, so they took a forward position and told the board to let them speak. This started a chain reaction throughout the crowd, so the school board responded by letting them speak. It was from that meeting onward that the NBPP began to take action in the school board meetings. At one point, they even shut down a school board meeting... It was at this meeting the community went up to the board members' seats and conducted their own school board meeting for the evening. This action changed the way the school board meetings were conducted and they proceeded to get the Dallas Police involved to regain control of the meetings. It was also at this time the current school board president, Bill Keever, began to prove his ineffectiveness for conducting

school board leadership and his board presidential duties.

The NBPP and the community called for his removal from office, due to the political positioning of the NBPP and the community at this time; the media began to attend the school board meetings and they began to get national press. Because of the NBPP's position on self-defense and discipline with small arms, Khallid Muhammad was visiting Dallas, Texas; he was introduced to the NBPP, whom he asked to handle his personal security. Khallid did not trust the NOI and needed an armed defense team that wasn't connected to religious ideology. It was this time that Aaron Michaels was introduced to Khallid Muhammad by way of another organization called the "Community Think-Tank," of which Hashim was a member. Aaron and Khallid began to forge a friendship and working relationship... Khallid Muhammed would always ask for the NBPP for his security if he was coming into the Dallas/ Ft. Worth area, which garnered the NBPP with local and national press because of the ideological differences Khallid had begun to talk about concerning many issues dealing with "White people" in general...

The NBPP had already established chapters in other cities including Indianapolis, Washington, D.C. Fort Worth, and Houston. We merged with the Panther Vanguard in L.A. after a meeting with the leadership in 1996 (Kwaku Duren, Boko Abar, and Tago) and

*formed the "New Panther Vanguard" movement.
This collective was short lived because at the same
time we were forming with the West Coast Panthers,
brothers and sisters on the East Coast wanted to join
and started working with Khalid Muhammad.*

*Khalid began to demand that people who joined
become "ultra-Black revolutionaries" and choose
sides with him because he was against Kwaku
because his wife was Anglo. We chose to work with
Khallid, and lost connection with Kwaku. Khallid
began to work with us as we started to make national
headlines, a move that would prove to be the catalyst
of failure on many levels within and outside the
ideology of the NBPP.*

*As we made national headlines with the church
burnings in Greenville, Texas, we continued to make
national press with ongoing issues within the Dallas
Independent School District and its school board.
After the murder of James Byrd Jr. in Jasper, Texas,
Aaron Michaels and the NBPP were about to make
the move into that city; Khallid Muhammad called
Aaron Michaels to make sure they showed up
together to deal with this situation; and Khallid
wanted to make sure he had a show of force with
armed NBPP members because he knew that's how
"we rolled"... This would solidify the NBPP in the
history books and on nightly television.*

*We went into the city to protect the community once
the police chief supported the KKK rally that was to*

take place in the Black community. This action called the NBPP into a defensive posture in protecting the African-American community. At this time, I was placed in charge of the maneuver under Aaron Michaels, I served as the Minister of Defense of Field Operations; it was at this time that I had my first clash with Khallid Muhammad. With him not understanding "Panther Protocol," he insisted to be head of the troops and serve as spokesman. This was against our structure and I told him he could not tell me how to coordinate the field operations. He then asked Aaron to remove me from the ranks!!! Aaron, of course, did not support him on this issue of my removal, but he did ask me to leave the room and Khallid was briefed on our structure by Aaron and David Foreman (The Dallas Chapter Chief of Staff).

It was also during the organizing of this event that I first meet Malik Zulu Shabazz who stood in as the Defense Attorney during the event. It was my penal code manual he used to review Texas Laws for the field actions in place. We also had Quanell X. on board from Houston, Texas as the community liaison for the maneuver. He eventually became the Chairman of the Houston Chapter, and once Aaron and Khallid decided that he needed to become a member of the NBPP if he wanted to have a voice within the organization then Quanell X. was appointed National Minister of Information. Aaron agreed to be the National Minister of Defense and "gave" Khallid the position of National Chairman.

In the structure that was in place prior to Khallid taking the NBPP National Chairmanship. But Aaron's and Khallid's power within the group was equally distributed; the Minister of Defense and Chairman had the same level of power. I, Aaron and David Foreman began to see the organization going into a different direction. The moment Khallid publicly announced his appointment, the organization began to grow exponentially. All the former NOI membership that supported Khallid left the ranks of the NOI and instantly became NBPP, without understanding "why they were joining" or the NBPP's internal structure.

We grew from organizing six chapters to over 20 chapters. This big jump in membership was great on the surface but came at a destructive cost. Consider the fact that Khallid's influence was so strong that masses of NOI membership religiously blindly followed Khallid from one uniform to the next, the NBPP was not based in religion and Khallid had to fill the void of this transition with a religious messiah leadership personality. In order to baby step this process Khallid started by changing the original 14-point platform of the NBPP to a 10-point platform with a "Spiritual Afrocentric Ideology" in order to allow a religious overtone to be employed and accepted when prior to this process, we did not have one in place.

Above, you see many of the reasons for the disarray of the NBPP, and its membership that is intrinsically lost, as it continues to stumble 11 years later after the death of Khallid Muhammad... Ladies and gentlemen, brothers and sisters, today is the day that you wake up and smell the coffee because it is burning on the stove!!!

And last of all, I never gave the leadership of the NBPP to Malik or Hashim; it was never theirs to try to lead or reshape. Malik Zulu Shabazz has never created any specific program or originated a true ideological platform in his life. As far as I can, tell he is a "community prostitute" and continues to whore the true ideas of the organization that I and others have created, and also diminishes the life and legacy of brothers and sisters from the African-American community and other struggles across the board. And when myself, David Foreman asked Hashim Nzingha to join the NBPP (before the cameras ever showed up in the hood and he saw stars, Hummers and cash signs rolling around in his head. He said that he wouldn't join because he "was afraid he might get shot." Now all of a sudden he's found the courage to be a great leader? Give me a freakin break... I doubt it very much he has that much courage!!! None of these brothers exhibit a clear understanding of the struggle of poor and oppressed people or an understanding of their own race's problems (whether they are economic, political, legal, military or otherwise.)

Dhoruba, once again this letter should have been written a long time ago; and because of the positioning of these "kneegros" and their fake-ass ideology, the NBPP has been listed as a terrorist group and not a "freedom fighting" organization working on behalf of people... To the caution of anyone thinking about working with this organization, I say to you, "Take your resources, your time and energy and work with organizations that are working for the freedom and liberation of all people including poor and oppressed people, and all people of color... Live up to the true creed of "ALL POWER TO THE PEOPLE!!!" Stay away from bullshit and anything that smells like bullshit... And when these two "kneegros" approach you for money, aid or a drink of water and say that they want it so they can help the people, you already know from their background and history with the AfricanAmerican community that they are lying; so don't waste your time...

PEACE!

Aaron Michaels,
Founder of The New Black Panther Party

After Dhoruba posted this, a little less than a month later on August 8, 2015, he and his group interrupted a conference the New Black Panther Party hosted at a downtown Atlanta hotel where the assault took place. This assault required Dhoruba, who was 71-years old at the time, and members of his group to have hospital attention. Dhoruba was the person injured the worst out of the group, which was roundly condemned by former members of the Black Panther Party, including those of us that truly represented the second generation Panther Movement in the 90s.

The differences between Revolutionary Nationalism, Spiritual Nationalism, and Cultural Nationalism became intertwined with Black Panther legacy and this new Black Muslim Movement named the New Black Panther Party as it stands today. In the book *"Liberation, Imagination and the Black Panther Party: A New Look at the Panthers and their Legacy"* by Kathleen Cleaver and George Katsiaficas, longtime political prisoner Mumia Abu-Jamal wrote about the "new Panther" emergence in the late 80s and early 90s with groups like ex-Black Panther Party cadre the Black United Liberation Front (BULF) out of Philadelphia (which became defunct after just six years), and the Sons of Malcolm also with ex-Black Panther Party cadre which ceased after just a few years. The St. Petersburg-based African People's Socialist Party (APSP) was led by longtime activist Omali Yesshitela (which Mumia described as more of a contemporary competitor organization than a successor formation). He also wrote about the controversial New Black Panther Party whose origin began in 1989 with radio talk show assistant Aaron Michaels in Dallas, Texas then later embracing the even more controversial former Nation of Islam official, Khalid Abdul Muhammad who Aaron would later hand over the reins of the

New Black Panther Party until the untimely death of Khalid who was then succeeded by Malik Zulu Shabazz. Mumia also mentions my group, the lower media profile New African American Vanguard Movement, later the New Panther Vanguard Movement, which also had ex-Black Panther Party cadre as part of its leadership. He is very complementary to the Vanguard regarding our growth and maturation along with our staying true to our platform and programs for the people as a continuation of the Panther Legacy. The other group Mumia mentioned was our New York comrades in the Black Panther Collective who also had ex-Black Panther Party cadre in its formation. For various reasons and some internal contractions, only the New Black Panther Party and the African Socialist People's remain from the 80s and 90s along with the recent emergence of groups like the Black Riders and the Huey P. Newton Gun Club who have sprung up in this era of Black Lives Matter.

As the above dialogue suggests, the New Black Panther Party has gone through a series of dramatic changes in personnel, philosophy, and theory. From my point of view, the New Black Panther Party presently is little more than the "unofficial" New Black Muslim Movement dressed like Pan– African "Panthers" while using the same rhetoric you would hear from an earlier era of the Nation of Islam. After the New York National Panther Summit and my return to Atlanta, Khalid and I would periodically call or meet at the First Afro Centric Temple to dialogue on various issues. Khalid and I, along with my wife, Kathy, developed a good friendship despite our differences and maintained that line of communication until his unexpected death on February 17, 2001 from a brain aneurism at an Atlanta hospital. I can say that I loved Brother Khalid and admired many of his qualities. But, in my opinion, he was never a "Panther" but needed to use that historical platform perspective not to appear at odds with the Nation of Islam which had a history of violence against defectors or former members like Malcolm X and others. Khalid understood how the Black community revered the Panthers, so until Aaron came along and after leaving the Nation, he was a man with a platform but had a respected constituency in the conscious community.

When all is said and done at this point, history will show that The New Black Panther Party hijacked the Black Panther Party legacy primarily with only a Platform but no true continuous programs for the people while the New Panther Vanguard Movement continued the positive legacy of the Black Panther Party without "gun posturing" and "media motivated" which was one of the major differences. Even with our lower profile, the New Panther Vanguard Movement accomplished a lot in the community with our programs to serve the people. This was our focus, not the media. I truly believe that back in our era in the 90s and up to this present time in 2016, that there are some good brothers and sisters in the present groups today including the New Black Panther Party. However, the August 8, 2015 beating of Dhoruba Bin Wahad and his group at an Atlanta hotel during a New Black Panther Party's Black Power Summit was very disturbing on many levels. To this date, no apologies or statements of regret have been issued. I truly believe had Khalid been alive, he would have never allowed Dhoruba and his group to be beaten. Despite Dhoruba disturbing their meeting, he would have allowed him to speak his mind to come to some conclusion and not order security to "get them out of here" by pummeling them. This resulted in Dhoruba having his jaw broken in four places and the others with injuries requiring going to the hospital. From the various reports I read, Malik Zulu Shabazz, who has an unmistakable Mobutu aura about him, was in total control of the meeting despite not being the "official" leader of the New Black Panther Party anymore and allowed the beating to take place. The New Black Panther Party Chief of Staff Chawn Kweli, who I like personally, did not give a satisfactory answer for the events that occurred that day, even though he has been the only New Black Panther Party leader to reach out to both generations of "Panthers" for counsel on various issues and is generally liked because of his humble, down to earth demeanor, unlike the others in this version of the New Black Panther Party. The actions that day were roundly condemned by first generation Panther as well as authentic second generation Panthers (New Panther Vanguard Movement and Black Panther Collective).

After reading Dhoruba's quotes along with statements by both Aaron Michaels and Robert

Williams, I could understand how the Dallas New Black Panther Party could be swayed by the aura of Khalid who was always very personable and persuasive. I believe there are some wonderful brothers and sisters in the New Black Panther Party despite the true intentions of their leadership.

Back to the Los Angeles Summit, Aaron was respectful and courteous on his visit but did not seem to be there when it came to implementing elements of our program in his organization. I believed he had his mind made up prior to his visit. Despite his programmatic disinterest, I felt that Kwaku and Shareef thought I had something to do with Aaron's lack of enthusiasm and wanted to have a private meeting about why Aaron was not down with our type of program and why he stayed with me initially. Our meeting would take place at Shareef's home involving Kwaku and myself. I automatically felt a "Goodie" move was going to be made against me and prepared myself for a debate for my very existence in the New Panther Vanguard Movement.

From Contradiction To Transformation _____

One of the early cracks in the foundation of the Vanguard Movement was when Goodie Williams left after having given so much of herself to the organization after our successful emergence in 1994. Toward the end of her tenure with the Vanguard, she was disempowered, became a castoff, and relegated to having very little influence within our organization despite having such a pivotal role in leadership during its inception. Goodie, Boko, Shareef, and Kwaku were the unquestioned leaders from the beginning. Others like me, Kizzy, Sheila, Simba, and Kwame took on a more supportive role within the organization. I always thought that the four primary leaders represented such a diverse leadership with each offering something different of value to the group which helped our early development. Kwaku had a wonderful way to explain theory and why we were organizing the people via our platform and programs. Shareef was the passion in the Vanguard and had one of the greatest speaking voices I have ever heard in person. Boko was the consciousness of the Vanguard with that Eternal Panther spirit of his. Goodie was the creative one of the initial leadership and was second only to Boko with organizing programs which Kizzy excelled at as well.

As time went on, there began to be disagreements and misunderstandings. Goodie would oppose Kwaku and Shareef on various issues which escalated to the point of Goodie's role within the organization being diminished. Perhaps the conflict was heightened by the fact that both Kwaku and Shareef were former members of the Black Panther Party and saw a vision of what direction and structure they wanted the organization to operate between the two of them with Goodie seeing a more collective decision making process. I have always thought that an organization that proclaimed "All Power to the People" would have that "power" reflected in its organizational structure which I believe caused some of the contradiction with Goodie. Boko was always the peacemaker and allowed people to work out their own issues, but Shareef and Kwaku were more hands on regarding implementation. Shortly after I became a member of the Vanguard's leadership council, Goodie was told to ask me about anything she wanted to do within the organization which was extraordinarily uncomfortable for me due to the fact that Goodie was a membership leader before me and it appeared that she was slowly being pushed aside. To say Goodie was important during our early development would be an understatement. She was a key figure in establishing the office along with Kwaku.

I hated to see this happen to such a dynamic person, regardless of the reason. I should have voiced my opposition to this treatment even more despite not knowing the extent of the issues. Excluding Boko, male machismo in leadership may have been a factor why Goodie's role diminished. She meant a lot to me, and it was painful to witness. Still, it caused a fundamental change in how I viewed roles with the Vanguard Movement. It was my train of thought that if you love the people, you need to have a love and regard for the people you worked with within that apparatus. I know I had much love and respect for Kwaku, Shareef, Goodie, and others within our group, especially Boko who became my mentor. I credit Kwaku and Shareef with developing my political maturation and for giving me the opportunity to serve the people with purpose. Boko taught me that serving the people is the greatest expression of love you could have for the community. While Goodie was not perfect and could cause issues from time to time, I really thought that she was a major part of our early success. The last time I saw Goodie was at her home after brain surgery, I made a point to tell her, "Goodie, I am glad that you were an example for me instead of me being an example for you". By this, I meant I would be ready for anything after witnessing what she went through.

To this day, I do not believe Kwaku and Shareef meant to harm Goodie in any way. Instead, I think they wanted a certain order within the organization without challenge because it meant that much to them. I understand that, but it was still wrong. I made sure that I stayed with Goodie up until I was preparing to leave Los Angeles in 1997. I was going through some of the same issues she faced during her time within the organization. As much as

I loved and respected Goodie, I was not her. I would not fly away like a bird by anyone unless I wanted to leave. This is something I never did until the end of the organization in the early 2000s. I told my wife, Kathy, who remembered Goodie's situation, that I was summoned to a meeting with Kwaku and Shareef and felt a "Goodie" move coming at this "members only" meeting. Kathy quickly reminded me that the $2,500 I raised to produce the first newspaper, *The Black Panther*, made her an "investor for life" member because she not only helped me with contacting "money" people as well as our savings but also the time it took for me initially to pound the pavement took away from our time in our new marriage. So, indeed, she insisted on coming to the meeting. I could not deny her point and there was no way I was going to stop her from attending. Plus, she knew how dedicated I was to serving the people despite some contradictions within the Vanguard.

On our way to the meeting at Shareef's residence, Kathy and I discussed how I now felt about everything that was happening in the organization. We also talked about whether or not I wanted to continue. I told her absolutely because there are times that you lose faith in people for various reasons, but I realized that good people can create a standard higher than the level of their own behavior. By following the Platform and Program instead of individuals, I was given a lifeline and the enthusiasm necessary to continue my work. Plus, Boko was always encouraging me to push through the contradiction. His logic was, where there is contradiction there can be transformation. Once we arrived at Shareef's house, Kathy told me, "I'll take Kwaku and you get Shareef. "We got this"! My wife has always had a confidence about her and was very protective of her new husband of one year, so it made me feel very confident as well even though I did not know what we were walking into. I anticipated a "debate" about Aaron, various issues, my place in leadership, and my continuing membership or not. In all honesty, I knew that my comrades, despite our issues, did not stand a chance with Kathy and me. I knew that my work within the organization was righteous and sincere but what hurt me within the apparatus is when I saw what Goodie went through. I stepped back from individuals but not my responsibilities within the Vanguard. Trust was always a big thing with me, and if I saw disloyalty within an organization, I feared that it would eventually become a "cancer" with members turning on each other or a "split" developing in the Panther Vanguard. This eventually did occur between Kwaku and Shareef when I lived in Atlanta. My reasoning was simply, if we say we love the people, then we need to love and show respect to those in the organization that serve the people.

Once inside Shareef's house, we all embraced then got right down to it. As planned, Kathy squared off with Kwaku and I had Shareef for our dialogue, which surprised both of them. Shareef did bring up the contradictions he had issues with concerning Aaron's arrival in Los Angeles, along with his disinterest toward the latter end of the Los Angeles Panther Summit, and why Aaron stayed at our place instead of his or Kwaku's. Because I was being truthful and had nothing to hide, I easily answered Shareef with reason and honesty by answering every question he had. I saw that he knew I was telling the truth. The conversation between Shareef and I was quite civil, but Kathy and Kwaku seemed to be really getting into what she perceived as my "major" contributions to the Vanguard, especially the money I raised for the first issue of *The Black Panther* newspaper. I sort of felt sorry for Kwaku, who was a brilliant debater. Still, I knew that Kathy was also an excellent debater, and when she saw blood, she went after it.

At one point during my dialogue with Shareef, we both stopped and became spectators as Kathy and Kwaku got louder. It even came to a moment when Kathy told Kwaku that if he did not think I was instrumental in the production of our newspaper then, "Give us back the $2,500 I raised for the organization and I want cash".

Kwaku's response was, *"Sister we don't have to go there"*. And Kathy's quick response was, *"Well, you went there"!*

Shareef and I had concluded our dialogue and came to an understanding but needed to play "referee" with Kathy and Kwaku. I rarely have seen Kwaku riled up, but Kathy had that "hot" Southwest Louisiana anger which I am fortunate to have seen only a few times in my life. At the end of the meeting, I remained in good standing with the organization as we embraced and shook hands. Shareef asked me if we were good. I said we were before Kathy added, "As long as he is good, I am good". With that, we left. To this day, I am not sure what Kwaku and Shareef intention was for me or what they truly wanted the end result to be, but it was clear, I was someone that could answer any contradiction with an answer of transformation. Kwaku and Shareef were instrumental in my political and social development and I am better for having had them in my life as a revolutionary activist. Still, I wish I could have been a "fly on the wall" when Kathy and I left Shareef's house.

I truly believed Kwaku and Shareef were committed to serving the people and building coalitions because it was evident in the tireless efforts and energy needed for leadership. Nevertheless, I had to get over my individual loyalty issues in order for me to move on knowing it could cause a problem later on even between the two of them. Whenever I had an issue with Kwaku or Shareef, it seemed to affect the relationship with many of the members they were close to. It also hurt some of the relationships with new members who went through the Ministry of Defense. My work schedule change to night shift, attending school, and absence from evening meetings while backing away from leadership caused a lack of building relationships with new members. I always got along with Sister Pat. She always treated me the same, and I developed somewhat of a healthy "comrade" crush on her because I truly admired the way she handled her business. She did not go along to get along. For a period of time, I handled the situation terribly. That was something I deeply regret, but it never stopped me from doing my duties. Building comradery within an organization is vital to its very existence and an essential ingredient in any movement that involved people working together for the community.

The younger members of the Vanguard like Dreamer Black, Bridgette, and Zahkee could have benefited even more by my consistent presence and by me spending more time talking to them. Shareef brought this up on a few occasions. I know he saw me backing away a bit after our "Goodie" issue, and I truly knew he wanted me to be re-entrenched within our organization as I had been in the beginning. Shareef was always more personable than Kwaku. It was not that Kwaku didn't get along with everyone, but it seemed that Shareef was more personal than political, and Kwaku was more political than personal. Despite personal issues, I had to salvage the relationships I moved away from and build new relationships because it was good for our organization in particular and the people we were serving in general. Adding emotion to the situation can prove to be detrimental when trying to go from contradiction to transformation by to taking things personally. This can help you avoid "jackanape" or non-cladestine mess ups. Back in the day during the Black Panther Party, a person was described as a "jackanape" if they were one who did not mean any harm but who would constantly "mess up". Their actions were not done as a suspected undercover agent trying to disrupt the organization. One of the contradictions I voiced was why the "other" ministries were not being developed and how new members who were now being indoctrinated through the Ministry of Defense and essentially staying there instead of training in the Defense Ministry for a period of time, then allowed to go to the Ministry of their interest or who the organization thought was a good fit for them.

One young brother (whose name I will not mention) that I brought into the organization personally had an altercation at the headquarters either with his fellow members of the Ministry of Defense or some associated people around the office. As a result of the altercation, he got beaten up pretty badly. To this day, it is not clear what happened, but the next day Shareef contacted me personally and apologized for the incident. He was aware that this young man had expressed interest in my area of responsibility, which was the Ministry of

Information. At the time, he was in the Ministry of Defense. Most of the brothers and sisters that were a part of the Defense Ministry came from the mean streets of South Central Los Angeles and were very tough so I understand Shareef's task to turn the "street" lumpen proletarians into revolutionary activists. This task had to take place in the Ministry of Defense, which I understood. However, this brother was more intellectual than a street soldier and was one who would always speak his mind. Brother Shareef made perfect sense explaining this to me and eventually the young brother left despite my efforts.

During our process, you lose good people who may not have been the best fit with a Ministry, but even I had to serve time in the security apparatus before being elevated to a position of leadership within the Vanguard. One thing you can count on is sure as you try to organize the people, "shit happens". It did, and we needed to move on. I never had any problem around some of these brothers due to my size – 6'2" and 230 pounds – or my being a part of the original leadership. I do also know that they loved Kathy, who always could put a smile on the face of the hardest brother. Many nights at the headquarters, I recall our "kickbacks" took place behind the office where Quadry was grilling or they happened when we all were sitting out back drinking a little "something, something". These were good times but every now and then, we would have to break up a fight over any issue that could turn a molehill into a mountain.   Once again, "Shit happens".

Sometimes the ladies would make plate lunches for fundraising, which involved the community and the Vanguard in a social environment. Both Shareef and Kwaku were great with our establishing a relationship with the community.   This included social events wherein we could interact with the people. Usually we did not have any conflict at the headquarters with the brothers. But I understood, like Shareef, where they were coming from because many came from places in impoverished areas of South Central.   All they knew in life was to fight and struggle. Many of our members were former members of the Blood and Crips gangs or former prisoners who were not far removed from the "jail" culture of survival. Even then, I felt like I could have spent more time with some of these brothers, but a move out of state would be in my immediate future.

My wife had expressed a desire to move closer to Louisiana so she could be nearer to her father, Velton a.k.a. Sonny, who lived in Scott, Louisiana where Kathy grew up.   I agreed and we started making plans to move in less than a year. During the final year in Los Angeles, I kept going to the office to take care of my responsibilities, but I missed many community forums because of my work and school schedule. I knew that my absence would bring up a point that I was again, separating myself. But at this time, that was not the case.   One of the most memorable events that occurred in my final year in

Los Angeles was when Geronimo Ji Jaga (also known as Elmer Pratt) was taken to Santa Ana for a bail hearing. There was not much to think he would be released due to the other court hearings we attended whenever he was brought to Los Angeles. This seemed to be a different type of day with the spirit of his supporters and comrades bellowing in the hallway in the courthouse. Geronimo had already served almost 28 years in prison as a victim of the government's COINTELPRO program, which J. Edgar Hoover was the architect. I recalled going down to the Santa Ana courthouse to cover his bail hearing for our newspaper, *The Black Panther*, so I went up to the floor where Geronimo's hearing was taking place. I must say it was amazing to see Emory Douglas, Eldridge Cleaver, and many supporters who, depending on who you were, could go into the actual courtroom to see Geronimo along with his legal team, which included his lawyer Johnny Cochran, legal counsel Kathleen Cleaver, and others.

At some point during this morning hearing, I noticed extra commotion and movement to and from the courtroom. A loud eruption took place inside the courtroom and people started celebrating after hearing that the judge had issued Geronimo to be released. As people filed out of the courtroom, I saw Emory who was wearing dreadlocks then and gave him a hug. He was smiling for days. I shook Geronimo's son's hand as he and the family filed out along with supporters, including Geronimo's wife at that time. Johnny Cochran emerged and tried to tell people that they were headed over to the holding area where Geronimo would be released. Because of the commotion, I don't think many people heard him. I did, so I followed Johnny and about eight other people to the holding center before everyone else figured out to go there. It blew my mind that I walked with those eight lawyers and was in the holding area waiting for Geronimo to come down the stairs as he would stride into freedom that day.

While in the holding area, I noticed Kathleen Cleaver and her ex-husband, Eldridge Cleaver, talking in two of the seats nearby. It appeared that they had not seen each other in a long time. I saw a very sensitive look on Eldridge's face. It was a far cry from the posters I had seen him in, and Kathleen was mostly listening to him. This would be one of the last times Kathleen would see her ex-husband, who would pass away in less than a year. When Geronimo emerged and took his strides down the stairs, there was so much excitement in the air, you could cut it with a knife. Geronimo embraced family, comrades, and well-wishers, including one of the original jurors who had voted guilty during his initial trial. Geronimo saw her and called her by name as he embraced her with a loving and forgiving hug. I stood about two feet from them hugging and took a picture of him being led out to supporters and media outside. The picture I took would go on the front page of our next issue of *the Black Panther* newspaper. Of course, I got no photo credit. Neelam was in charge of the paper by that time. I had to work that night, so I was not able to go to Reverend Cecil "Chip" Murray's church where the celebration would take place. I hated to miss out, but I did my job on one of the most exciting days I have witnessed to this day.

Just before I was to leave Los Angeles for Atlanta in the summer of 1997, Kwaku had summoned me to Panther International Headquarters and asked if I could keep Kathy at home this time. I couldn't blame him after our last encounter with me, Kathy, Kwaku and Shareef. Upon arriving at our headquarters at Panther International, Kwaku and I sat in the law office side of our building and talked about my pulling back from individuals, but supporting the collective organization overall. I also would participate in events and programs, but was either going alone or with Boko, who, by then, was my full-fledged mentor. Kwaku correctly brought up some of my impersonal behavior at times and I explained the mistrust I had developed because of some contradictions I saw going on organizationally along with a work schedule that further caused issues since I was not able to attend many leadership meetings. Kwaku told me that at one of the meetings, from which Boko was absent, there was some dialogue about whether or not I should even be in the organization at all when I moved to Atlanta.

Kwaku and I further discussed the issues I had with him, Shareef and now Neelam, who had become a major part of the organization as his "new" wife with an opinion that reflected her new position organizationally. I never had a big problem with Neelam, who became more assertive. But I felt that as an "OV" a.k.a. Original Vanguard Panther before Kwaku even knew Neelam, I deserved the respect for what I had contributed from the beginning. I did not feel the need to answer to her. Being a Pan-Africanist and a Black Nationalist by nature, I wanted the Panther Vanguard to be "All Black" anyway. And having an East Indian Londoner who was instantly empowered within a so-called "Black" organization was an adjustment for me from a personal perspective. Nevertheless, I would be lying to say Neelam was not good for the group because of what she brought to the table skill wise. By the time of my meeting with Kwaku, Neelam had taken control of our newspaper, *The Black Panther*. She did a great job, having previously been a part of the London paper called *Panther,* which was produced by the Black and Asian organization there. Still, I felt she needed to stay out of my business, nonetheless.

I discussed with Kwaku my plans after my Atlanta move and had already purchased an airline ticket to Chicago to work on the "Free Fred Hampton, Jr." campaign that his mother, Akua Njeri, was the architect. I also brought up the Goodie issue I had and how I thought we had moved on from that. We also talked about how me being in Atlanta and Kamau Osiris being in Indianapolis gave us representation on the East Coast and the Midwest, which was good for the Vanguard. I thought the coalition work I would be continuing which I excelled at, coupled with a national presence gave him enough intrigue to see those possibilities. For the second time, we agreed to keep moving forward together and shook hands as I left. Boko eventually heard about the meeting and was not pleased that I went through this again. Had it not been for Boko and my wife, I would not have survived my membership in the New Panther Vanguard Movement. Boko was a consistent supporter and comrade of mine. He truly believed I was moving to Atlanta because of the issues with the top of our hierarchy. This was not the reason, but it did allow me the freedom without contradictions waged against me.

A day before I was to leave with my wife in a rented UHaul, Boko came to help me load the truck and say goodbye. I remember smiling when I saw him wearing his cut jeans shorts the way we wore them in Louisiana and how he wore them as a kid in Houston. Later Boko would fly to Chicago to support the Free Fred Hampton, Jr. campaign and then come to Atlanta for events. So I got to see my mentor quite a few times before he actually moved to Atlanta after meeting his future wife Akilah Shukura Nosakhere who worked for the Auburn Avenue Research Library on African-American History. She was also a key organizer when we worked on the "Panther" events in Atlanta like the conferences, photo exhibits, and panel discussions we had at the library. Boko and Akilah actually met at a reparations conference and have never been apart since then.

Despite our ups and downs, I would not be who I am today without Kwaku and Shareef being a part of my life. I am forever indebted to them for allowing me to "Serve the People" with the Panther Vanguard Movement. For this, they will always be heroes of mine. Our relationship was not the best at times, but I made sure I told them personally how important they were to me and both seemed to appreciate me telling them that. It is said, "Absence makes the heart grow fonder," and that is how it played out between Malik, Shareef and Kwaku. As I continued my Vanguard work in Atlanta and nationally, I felt that they had regained an appreciation for me and saw I was committed to the people. In 2002, I heard a fire at the headquarters impacted the means of production of the organization. Then, I heard about a split within the organization between Kwaku and Shareef. I don't know what happened to cause this, but it was damaging to our organization. By the time of reconciliation, we were already headed towards our demise. As unclear as our demise was, it still hurt because organizationally we were on target as a movement. Yet, we created a standard higher than the level of our own behavior at times.

I remained with the organization until its end in late 2002. I was proud of the fact that we accomplished a lot without much fanfare or controversy. The Panther Vanguard truly picked up the torch of the Black Panther legacy by serving the people through community programs and stiffening the resistance to oppression while establishing multicultural coalitions in direct opposition to the system of oppression. There was a lot to consider with us emerging from Los Angeles: half of the comrades in the Black Panther Party murdered were from the Southern California Chapter of the Black Panther Party; the survivors of the police invaded their office at 41st and Central; the assassinations of Bunchy Carter and John Huggins; the framing of Geronimo Ji Jaga; the chapter eventually close after Geronimo went to jail. Between 1976-1981, the re-opening of the Black Panther Party chapter by Kwaku was located in Southern California. In 1994, the emergence of the Panther Vanguard was founded by three former Black Panther Party members. This "authentic" second generation Panther movement could not have taken place anywhere else. Yes, there were "Panther" type organizations around prior to our emergence, but I regard most of them as "Hair and Nail Shop Revolutionaries" or panther gun toting cheerleaders absent of any programs for the people. Bobby Seale was quoted, "The Black Panther Party was a social, evolutionary accident that took civil disobedience to the cutting edge: and The Vanguard did the same as revolutionary activists during our era. A few years after our demise, Kwaku called me to let me know he would be coming to Atlanta for a reparations conference. He wanted us to meet and that made me very happy to see Kwaku after years of not seeing him, and he still amazed me with his energy and vitality. After the reparations conference I attended with him, I asked him to come by our house. He complied, and we sat and talked for hours. After the drinks and conversation, he departed back to his hotel room, even though we offered to let him spend the night. It meant the world to me for him to come visit and spend time with me and my wife. I then remembered why I followed such a dynamic duo in Kwaku and Shareef despite our issues and how much we accomplished during our era. Of course, Boko, the Eternal Panther, remained my comrade and friend throughout the years as well as Kamau Osiris. I am equally indebted to both of them. I never got to see Shareef again because he died of stage four cancer on March 21, 2015 with his wife Weetie Abdullah, family, and Kwaku by his side. His death rocked all of us, but especially those who saw him in Los Angeles in those last few years.

Shareef and I had been communicating via email and Facebook to check on each other. He told me how proud he was of me and my wife telling me it truly "takes two". Boko encouraged me in so many ways beyond being a revolutionary activist. Shareef and Kwaku spearheaded my writings for years to come. I give complete credit to them for giving me a voice for the people via my articles. Some mistakes were made along the way, but like the Watts Riots in 1965, the Panther Vanguard rose like a phoenix after the Rodney King Rebellion. We changed the landscape for the better. I truly learned that without contradiction, there could be no transformation because when our people were backed into a corner, we came out like the Panthers we are. Not only were we noticed by the people, but our first generation Panthers took notice and gave us the salute of All Power to the People.

The Panther Reunions_____

The first Black Panther Reunion I attended was held in Oakland, California on October 12, 1996. It commemorated the 30th anniversary of the Black Panther, which was sponsored by It's About Time Commemorating Committee under the direction of Billy X Jennings. The Vanguard Movement emerged just two years prior to this event and had recently published the first edition of *The Black Panther News Service*, which we brought to sell during the events of that weekend's festivities. As Kathy and I walked into the first session of the reunion, I observed a "who's who" of the Black Panther Party in the room.

One of the first people I recognized was Kathleen Cleaver. She was seated next to David DuBois, a former editor of *The Black Panther* newspaper for a while during the era of the Party. I walked over to Kathleen and introduced myself. I then told Kathleen what organization I was a part of and she was already familiar with the Vanguard.

Kathleen stood up and gave me a hug then expressed how it was nice to meet me. I am not a presumptuous person, but I thought she had probably heard my name before since our October 1994 emergence. This was the first time I met Kathleen in person although I had admired her for a long time prior to this encounter. Kathleen was well respected by most Party members, even during the most difficult periods of the Black Panther Party. She was one of the most articulate people I had ever heard during the many news clips of that era. In terms of eloquence, Kathleen reminded me of Malcolm X in many ways because of her intellectual clarity when she spoke.

During the 60s and 70s, many Black Panther spokesmen would curse during speeches but I never recalled hearing any audio or video of Kathleen using vulgarity. I truly admired her for that. I did see Kathleen at a press conference supporting a new trial for Geronimo Ji Jaga in Los Angeles which included the likes of Celeste King of the Los Angeles chapter of the Congress of Racial Equality, Rapper YoYo, Compton Mayor Omar Bradley, actor Mike Farrell, and Avatar Records President Larry Robinson, who presented Kathleen and the Geronimo Committee a check for $10,000. The Vanguard Movement was there as well, and whenever Geronimo was brought to Los Angeles or areas nearby, we always made a strong showing of support. When I moved to Atlanta, I would see Kathleen either at an event like a Black Panther Reunion, The Emory Douglas Art Exhibit (which included the Art and Culture Conference of the Black Panther Party held at the Auburn Avenue Research Library), and the Southwest Arts Center which was organized by the It's About Time Committee. Boko, Kamau, and I would assist Billy X when certain events were held in Atlanta or if she had a book signing. For example, Boko and I attended a book signing at The Shrine of the Black Madonna Bookstore for her book, *Liberation, Imagination and the Black Panther Party*. Kathleen was always very cordial, but she held me at arm's length even though we both lived in Atlanta. I imagined that maybe because she did not really know me or maybe because I had the title of Minister of Information for the New Panther Vanguard Movement's second generation Panthers while her ex-husband, Eldridge Cleaver, is the iconic image of that Panther title. This may have been, from her perspective, an infringement on her husband's legacy. I don't know. All I know is that I have always had the highest regard for Kathleen and was very happy to see her at the Stanley Nelson Atlanta film premier of "The Black Panthers: Vanguard of the Revolution" where we got to take a picture together.

Interestingly, when we hosted a highly successful Art and Culture Conference of the Black Panther Party with the Emory Douglas Art Exhibit, I had the opportunity to meet Robert Hillary King, a member of the Angola 3. The other two members (Albert Woodfox and the late Herman Wallace) and Robert King were former member of the Black Panther Party. Robert spent 32 years of which 29 years in solitary confinement. I had the opportunity to meet him at the Southwest Arts Center where we held the exhibit but did not get to speak with him very long. I asked my cousin Jeff if I could borrow a few of the family newsletters. After reviewing them at home, I saw Robert Hillary King's picture and advertisement of his book, *From the Bottom of the Heap*, in the family news. I never connected Robert's last name (King) with my family in Delhi, Louisiana, him being one of the Angola 3 with him possibly being my relative on my father's side of the family – James Robinson, who come from Delhi/

Rayville, Monroe area of Northern Louisiana. During our Vanguard era, we supported Billy X, who always visited and supported the Angola 3. Still, I never knew until recently that Robert Hillary King and I are blood relatives. I joined a successor Black Panther formation and he was an imprisoned member of the Black Panther Party. We both are authors with me coincidentally writing my first book, *From Old Guard to Vanguard: A Second Generation Panther*. This makes me think that history does not evolve without a sense of irony. I look forward to seeing Robert at the 50th anniversary of the Black Panther Party this year- a true family reunion!

Billy X Jennings has to be credited with uniting former Black Panther Party members through these reunions and conferences. As the Black Panther Party's chief archivist, he has been instrumental in a resurgence of the legacy of the Black Panther Party along with the support and participation of his wonderful wife, Gail. Billy X set up an outstanding website that highlights the past accomplishments of the Party. I look forward to events that celebrate the Party. One of the most heartfelt sections of the website is the tribute to fallen comrades, which features history of the deceased comrades along with support for the family. Billy was always a big advocate of the Panther Vanguard and supported whatever event we organized including features in the It's About Time Commemorative Committee's newsletter that Billy produced to keep all Panthers in the know with information. I have even had a feature or two in the newsletter myself. In turn, any event that Billy had going on would be carried in our version of *The Black Panther* newspaper.

The New Panther Vanguard Movement is widely regarded by first generation Panthers as their second generation, not just because we had former Black Panther Party members in our cadre, but the work in the community was highly respected by not only these first generation Panthers, but even Bobby Seale has credited the New Panther Vanguard Movement with carrying the Black Panther Party legacy forward. He has been quoted as saying, "The Los Angeles Panthers are on target". Billy is quoted often when mentioning the Vanguard by saying, "The Black Panther Party didn't stop in 1980, and *The Black Panther* newspaper did not stop in 1980". During Billy's Black Panther Party Photo Exhibits, the New Panther Vanguard Movement is the only 90s "Panther group" with a display to be shown to the public, showing the legacy of "Serving the People" was continued in the 90s. The only other group that the first generation Panthers are recognized by in large was the Black Panther Collective in New York which was also composed of former Black Panther Party members.

The other It's About Time event I attended was the 35th anniversary of the Black Panther Party, held in Washington, D.C. at the University of the District of Columbia campus in 2001. This reunion would be the last time I saw Michael Zinzun, a Pasadena Black Panther who later became a key person in bringing the Crips and Bloods together via a gang truce. Michael was co-founder of the Coalition Against Police Abuse (CAPA) with Kwaku Duren, our Chairman. I saw him often at the Coalition Against Police Abuse office. His untimely death sent shockwaves through the Panther alumni. He is greatly missed. Many traveled from near and far to attend this historic event. The highlight was the many workshops where the dialogue was outstanding. Of course, the New Black Panther Party, led by Malik Zulu Shabazz had to make their presence known to all who attended. Malik and his group were stopped at the door by Billy X and given instruction on how they would behave once inside. Then they were allowed to enter, and they did so without any issue.

On October 20-23, 2016, The Black Panther Party will celebrate its 50th anniversary in Oakland, California, where it all began in 1966. There is much anticipation leading up to this historic golden anniversary event. The reunion should be covered nationally and internationally by the media, and I am looking forward to the festivities myself. Many of the first generation Panthers are still living and continue to contribute to the struggle. The 50th anniversary may be the last "golden anniversary" celebration given the fact that many are in their 60s, 70s and 80s, so I will cherish seeing many of them. I don't think they will be around for a 75th anniversary celebration. Actually, I don't even know if I will be around either at the age of 76 when that golden anniversary arrives. I often think about Bobby Seale, Kathleen Cleaver, Elaine Brown, Ericka Huggins, Big Man Howard, Emory Douglas, Kwaku, Shareef, Boko, Ronald and Roland Freeman, Wayne Pharr, Akua Njeri, Billy X, and others as the true heroes of the people. I feel fortunate to have known many of them. Most within the hierarchy of the Black Panther Party would say that the true heroes of the People and the Party were the "Rank and File" members of the Black Panther Party who did the everyday work. This is also true of the Panther Vanguard Movement during our era as well. Whenever I attended these reunions or helped organize them with Billy and It's About Time, I always witnessed a spirit of great love for the people and soaked it up each time. The attendees represented the entire spectrum of race, colors, and creeds. This was a testament to how the Black Panther Party brought people together. Because of my Los Angeles indoctrination, I think of those Los Angeles Black Panther Party members from the first generation, especially Ronald and Roland Freeman, along with Wayne Pharr, who can be seen in much of the Vanguard's film footage during our events or programs where they often spoke. Those specific three have joined the ancestors, and I still think of them fondly. That's why it is so important for the Black Panther Party members and supporters to recognize their history through celebration because they did not do it for the fame or notoriety but to "Serve the People – Body and Soul". The Panther Vanguard Movement was proud to carry on the tradition of revolutionary activism. And, yes, there was a Second Generation Panther in the 90s worth celebrating as well. All Power to the People and Panther Power to the Vanguard!

Charles "Boko" Freeman:
The Eternal Panther _____

Charles "Boko" Freeman was born and raised in Houston, Texas. In 1967, Charles left Houston for New York. In New York, Charles attended Andrew Jackson High School where he was active in the Black Student Union. He was introduced to the speeches of Malcolm X and later became active as a community worker with the Queens chapter of the Black Panther Party. Charles returned to Houston in 1969 with plans of organizing a chapter of the Black Panther Party in Houston. Surprisingly, he met another young activist with the same idea. His name was Carl Hampton. He and Charles would become fast friends and close comrades.

Like Charles, Carl Hampton was encouraged to return to Houston, Texas to establish a chapter there. Hampton had worked with the Black Panther Party in Oakland, California where he, like Charles, was inspired by the philosophy and activity of the Black Panther Party.

By the spring of 1970, Charles Freeman, Carl Hampton, and others formed a community group modeled after the Black Panther Party. However, they were not permitted to become an official. The explosive growth of the Black Panther Party overwhelmed the management capabilities of central leadership, and a freeze was issued to suspend the founding of new chapters for a time.

Undaunted by this order, the group named itself **People's Party II** in recognition of the Black Panther Party as the "first People's Party". Within eight weeks after the opening of the People's Party II, an armed standoff occurred between People's Party II members and the Houston Police Department (HPD). On July 26, 1970, the Houston Police Department in collusion with federal authorities carried out the assassination of Carl Bernard Hampton, who was recognized as one of the most dynamic young revolutionary Black leaders in America.

The tragic loss of Carl Hampton was felt by the fledging organization and the community at large. Nevertheless, the community work continued under the guidance of Charles Freeman and James Aaron. In the tradition of Black Panther community programs across the country, the People's Party II provided free breakfast for children, food for families, clothing, medical screenings, and pest control services for the community.

In recognition of Carl Hampton's supreme sacrifice, the central committee of the Black Panther Party granted chapter status to People's Party II and officially, it became known as the Houston Texas Chapter of the Black Panther Party. The Houston chapter continued its activities until 1974 when all members were summoned to central headquarters in Oakland, California in a move to consolidate Panther operations to one location.

After a few weeks of life as a Panther in Oakland, Charles left the Party citing growing ideological differences and concerns for his personal safety. He resettled in Los Angeles to establish himself. He made several attempts to re-activate his membership but was rebuffed by new Panther leadership.

In 1978, Bob Kwaku Duren, a Black Panther, spearheaded the reopening of the Southern California chapter to reestablish Panther community services and programs. Charles joined this effort and quickly became a skilled organizer of mass food giveaways, public events, rallies, forums, and festivals. The Southern California chapter of the Black Panther Party is believed to be the last chapter in the country to disband, not realizing that the central headquarters had ceased to exist.

Disappointed and disillusioned by the demise of the Black Panther Party, Charles devoted the following years to his family, his spiritual life, and development of his commercial art business in the Los Angeles area. Still, his innate desire to serve his community remained foremost in his heart. As the result of his spiritual studies and eventual initiations, Charles Freeman became known as 'Boko Abar.'

The Black Panther Party had been defunct for over a decade when Boko called B. Kwaku Duren to share his idea of a rebirth of the organization. Surprisingly, Kwaku and another veteran Panther, Shareef Abdullah, were thinking along the same line and had been meeting with a small group in Compton for several weeks.

In 1994, continued discussion and contemplation between the three men (all veterans of the original Black Panther Party) founded the "New African American Vanguard Movement". The name was later changed to the "New Panther Vanguard Movement". The official inauguration was set for October 1994 to coincide with the October founding date of the original Black Panther Party 28 years earlier.

The rebirth of the Black Panther Party as the New Panther Vanguard Movement was publicly introduced in Leimert Park at Marla Gibbs Vision Theatre. Over 700 people attended the festive celebration that included live entertainment, public speakers, and the giveaway of 1,000 bags of groceries.

The New Panther Vanguard Movement (NPVM) headquarters was located at 1470 Marin Luther King, Jr. Boulevard in south central Los Angeles. In 1996, a new quarterly edition of the famous *Black Panther* newspaper was republished to inform the public of international freedom movements, the needs of political prisoners, as well as the revised Ten Point Platform and Program of the New Panther Vanguard Movement and ongoing programs. The growth of the New Panther Vanguard Movement continued steadily until 2002 when the headquarters suffered an explosion and fire that closed the building for a time. Renovation of the building became problematic and proved detrimental to the continuation of the organization's base of operation. Today, the future of the New Panther Vanguard Movement is in limbo as the Black Panthers experience yet another setback. In 1997, Boko returned to Houston to commemorate the life of fellow activist Carl Bernard Hampton with a festival and free food giveaway for the needy of Houston. Houston Police assassinated Hampton, the founder of the Peoples' Party II on July 26, 1970. It was Boko's desire to insure the memory of a young Black revolutionary that, without fear, confronted injustice and is not forgotten by Houston and the world.

Long Live the Revolutionary Spirit of Carl B. Hampton, Charles Boko Freeman, and The Panther Vanguard Movement. All Power to the People!

My Writings, Travels And Opinions_____

Chicago Founder Jean Baptist Point DuSable

A little known fact outside of Chicago is that this great city was founded by a Black man. Haitian fur trader and business man Jean Baptist Point DuSable was the first to settle the area that would become known as Chicago. This has been Chicago's little secret for generations of its inhabitants and least known to the rest of the nation as it is commonly regarded as America's "Second City". DuSable is the earliest recorded resident of the settlement close to the mouth of the Chicago River that grew to become the city of Chicago. He is, therefore, regarded as the first permanent resident of Chicago and given the appellation "Father of Chicago".

Jean Baptiste Point DuSable settled on the north bank of the Chicago River sometime in the 1780s. He was first recorded living in Chicago around early 1790. Point DuSable, an AfricanCaribbean, was born in St. Marc, Haiti in around 1745 and died August 28, 1818 in St. Charles, Missouri near St. Louis. In Chicago, a school, museum, harbor, park, and bridge have been named or renamed in his honor. The place where he settled at the mouth of the Chicago River in the 1780s is recognized as a National Historic Landmark, now located in Pioneer Court where a bust is prominently displayed. The sculptor of the DuSable bust is Erik Blome, and the monument was installed there in 2009.

Point DuSable married a Potawatomi Indian woman named Catherine in English or Kitty Hawk in her native culture in the 1770s. She would bear him a son named Jean and a daughter named Susanne. Jean Baptiste Point DuSable was described by British Commandant Arent DePeyster at Fort Michlilmackinac (1774-1779) as handsome, well-educated and settled in Eschecagou. He was a skilled business man in the tradition of French commerce and because of his manner, he was well respected. DuSable seemed to really prosper in the future named Chicago, but for many speculative reasons, he abruptly left Chicago in 1800.

Many claim that perhaps his failed attempt to become a chieftain in his wife's Potawatomi Tribe may have discouraged him. Or, if he could have been that the reported death of his wife led to his leaving. Perhaps the 1795 Treaty of Greenville and the subsequent westward migration of Indians away from the Chicago area might have played a part in his exit. Maybe the fact that Point DuSable was angered that the United States Government wanted to buy the land on which he lived and called his own for the previous two decades may have been a factor. Who really knows? But what became of his territory would evolve into the great metropolis in the nation's center. I am not sure that DuSable could imagine

Chicago would become a Black metropolis with the highest concentration of Blacks in the nation. This man would establish the first house, trading post, and homesteads. He was the area's first Catholic who would become the only person to see the commercial possibilities of Chicago.

The legacy of what Jean Baptiste Point DuSable started in Chicago would become a vibrant city of music, culture, sports, Black business, art, and political influence that would affect the entire nation and the world with its achievement. It went from the worldwide spectacle of the 1893 Chicago's World Fair (otherwise known as the World's Columbian Exposition) that brought unprecedented attention to this emerging metropolis with thousands of visitors descending on the city. This historic World Fair would attract many from all sectors of society including social reformers Abolitionist Frederick Douglass, journalist Ida B. Wells, women's rights pioneer Susan B. Anthony, editors Irvine Garland, and Ferdinand Lee Barnett. In 1933, Chicago hosted another World's Fair with the motto, "A Century of Progress in Technological Innovation". This fair attracted many including Robert Sengstacke Abbott from Georgia who would relocate to Chicago shortly after his visit to this mega fair. Abbott, a lawyer by trade, established *The Chicago Defender* newspaper, which focused on the AfricanAmerican community. *The Chicago Defender* would attract the writing talents of Langston Hughes, Gwendolyn Brooks, and Willard Motely in a city full of creative writers and playwrights like Richard Wright and Lorraine Hansberry.

The prominence of African-American achievement in the city of Chicago can be credited to the entrepreneurial spirit of Jean Baptiste Point DuSable as Blacks have reached heights never reached before in much of the country. Legends have emerged from the Black Metropolis of Chicago in fields like politics. They are represented by the likes of Harold Washington, Jesse Jackson, Minister Louis Farrakhan, Carol Moseley Braun, Fred Hampton of the Black Panther Party, and, of course, Chicago developed the political maturation of our 44th President, Barak Obama.

Excellence in the powerful Black Arts and Culture Movement would be represented by people like Haki Madhubuti, Dr. Margaret Burroughs, Romare Bearden, Jacob Lawrence, Marva Jolly, and others. In music, it is too numerous to mention all those from DuSable's Chicago, but names like Gospel originator Thomas A. Dorsey, who wrote the classic "Precious Lord", and great gospel singer Mahalia Jackson need to be mentioned. In the secular music field, legends like Curtis Mayfield of the Impressions, The Staple Singers, Donnie Hathaway, Minnie Ripperton, Rotary Connection, Chaka Khan, Coco Taylor, Earth Wind & Fire, Jerry Butler, Sam Cooke, Buddy Guy, recently passed House Music Godfather Frankie Knuckles, Laila Hathaway, R. Kelly, and many more provide the musical fabric of Chicago along with the famous

"Steppin" dance craze on the South and West side of Chicago in popular Black areas like historic Bronzeville.

Black aviation also became very popular in Chicago with the likes of Col. John Robinson – who fought for Ethiopia against Italy. Ethiopia remains the only African country never to be colonized. Black aviation pioneers Bessie Coleman, Willa Brown, Cornelius Coffey, and many young men who would go on to become Tuskegee Airmen are also part of the Chicago fabric. In the commerce tradition of Point DuSable, Chicago would produce some of the country's most prominent leaders in business and media with the likes of John H. Johnson of Johnson Publishing Company and his wife Linda Johnson, as well as Oprah Winfrey, Earl Graves, and Munson Steed of the Steed Media Group that produces *rolling out* magazine. Certainly, the entrepreneurial spirit of Jean Baptist Point DuSable planted a seed that continued to grow after his departure from Chicago.

Despite establishing such a tremendous historical legacy, for a long time the city did not honor DuSable in the same manner as other pioneers. Chicago commemorated Point DuSable's homestead in 1913 with a plaque on the corner of Kinzie and Pine Streets. In 1933, at Century of Progress International Exposition, a number of African-American groups campaigned for Point DuSable to be honored at the fair. At this time, few Chicagoans had even heard of DuSable, and the fair's organizers were presented the 1803 construction plans of Fort

Dearborn where DuSable's homestead was located as the city's historical beginning. This effort was successful and a replica of his cabin was presented as part of the background of the history of Chicago during the exposition. In 1965, Pioneer Court Plaza was built on the site of Point DuSable's homestead as part of the construction of the Equitable Life Insurance Society of America building. The Jean Baptiste Point DuSable Home site was designated as a National Historic Landmark on May 11, 1976 until established at the current Pioneer Court at 401 North Michigan Avenue in the near North Side of Chicago. In 2009, the City of Chicago and a private donor financed a bronze bust to commemorate Chicago's Black Founder "DuSable".

"The Hunt is on and (Black People) you are the Prey" _____

These eloquently haunting words were articulated by actor Charles S. Dutton in the 1993 film "Menace II Society," which showed the plight of young Black men growing up in America, who are regarded by police as Target Zero.

The historical reality of police violence against Blacks, the poor, and people of color has been an age old problem that has been highlighted recently with the killings of Mike Brown, Eric Gardner, John Crawford, Kajieme Powell, Tamir Rice, and those "playing police" with George Zimmerman's murder of Trayvon Martin. The public outrage over these killings has brought unprecedented attention on the relationship between the police department and communities of color for decades as police are more willing to shoot first and answer questions later. The police motto of "protect and serve" seems to have been thrown out the window and replaced with "patrol and control" as the principle tactic used in urban communities.

Police officers cannot "protect and serve" a community that they fear or have hatred for in urban neighborhoods, public places or in street confrontations. Many of the assigned officers in our communities don't live there and fail to understand the residents who they view as a law-less criminal element.

Though cultural training to officers patrolling these communities can be effective, I believe that officers from that community will best understand the community they patrol since they have a vested interest in it. If other officers are coming into our community from other ethnic communities, they should at least have a partner from that community or similar ethnic neighborhood. Indeed, there are police officers of various races that do a good job of protecting and serving regardless of race, but the problems of a community are best understood by someone from that community.

Adding a historical perspective, back in the late 1950s Malcolm X battled against police brutality in the 1957 case of Johnson X Hinton. In his Queens home the following year, it was in late April 1962 that Malcolm X faced what many cite as the greatest tragedy of his tenure with the Nation of Islam. In what journalist Peter Goldman termed "a sort of volte-face version of the Johnson parable", Los Angeles police accosted several Mosque 27 members who were unloading dry cleaning from their car. The officers were suspicious due to a chain of clothing store burglaries in the area and confronted the men. A scuffle ensued, the details of which are still muddled.

However, after what *The Los Angeles Times* later dubbed a "blazing gunfight" despite the fact that none of the Muslims were armed, seven mosque members were shot, many through the back. One was paralyzed, another five were injured, and most dramatically, Korean War veteran and mosque secretary Ronald X Stokes was shot and killed at close range while walking towards an officer with his hands raised. The Black Panther Party's first issue of the group's newspaper, *The Black Panther*, publicized the Richmond California Police murder of Denzil Dowell whose autopsy showed that he was shot in his torso and armpits. It was clear that his arms were up when he was shot.

The listing of police murders of unarmed Black citizens runs deep. Let me provide a short list of some of the most egregious killings such as the 1970 killing of Vietnam War Vet Jerry Lee Amie, who was shot 24 times in front of his home in Los Angeles. This was witnessed by his mother and sister while his hands were raised. Also in Los Angeles during the 1970s, William Gavin was shot 22 times by the Los Angeles Police Department. Across the country in Miami, Arthur McDuffie was being beaten to death by police officers after a "chase" in which he was riding his bike. This sparked the 1980 Miami Riots. The Philadelphia Police dropped a bomb on the home of the MOVE Organization in 1985, resulting in 11 deaths including children. Malice Green in Detroit was killed by police while in custody listing flashlights as the weapon.

Eleanor Bumpers was killed during an eviction after getting four months behind in rent. She was shot by an officer with two blasts from a 12-gage shot gun. The New York City Police abuse of Abner Louima in 1997 where Louima was beaten by police in a precinct bathroom and had a broken broom inserted in his rectum then jammed in his mouth, breaking his teeth.   Tyisha Miller in Riverside, California was shot 23 times while in her car that had a flat tire and was parked at a filling station until her family could arrive after calling the Riverside Police Department in 1998.   Then there was the shooting of Amadu Diallo in New York City.   He was killed by four New York City cops died in a barrage of 41 shots after pulling his wallet out of his pocket in front of his brownstone.

Also in New York, Black undercover officers working the subway were being shot by fellow White officers after being mistaken as criminals.   In 1994, Desmond Robinson, a Black undercover officer was shot four times and severely injured by fellow officer Peter Del-Debbio, a White officer.   The shooting provoked a highly charged public debate over whether White officers were too quick to assume that Black undercover officers were criminals.

Other similar cases of Black undercover officers being shot by their White counterparts are numerous but interestingly, no White undercover officer has ever shot by a Black undercover officer while working the New York City subway.   The infamous cases of elderly citizens Oscar Grant in Oakland and Kathryn Johnson in Atlanta cannot be overlooked.   Ms. Jackson was a 92-year old Black grandmother who was shot down in a hail of 39 shots with six bullets during a "botched" police drug raid November 2006. I don't think a White grandmother in a White community would have been treated with such disregard for her life.

Race is very much a part of this conflict with the Militarization of Police Departments assigned to communities of color, especially the Black community. Raids by Special Weapons and Tactics (SWAT) teams are up 1,400% since the 1980s.

According to Pundit Fact Statistical data, 99% of the time, police officers aren't charged when they kill young people of color. Homicide is the #1 killer of young Black men between 15-34 years old. Race is very much a part of this long standing issue between the Black community and police department, the local military arm of the power structure. In the midst of these tragic incidents, people of all colors, including some Black and White police officers, have stood up to say this is wrong. In 1896, the Plessy vs. Ferguson determined legally that a Black man (or woman) had no rights that a White man was bond to respect. But people of this era are saying in unison, "BLACK LIVES MATTER. END THIS
HUNT!"

The Unholy Union:
The FBI & Its Black Informants

The recent allegations against Black leader, Rev. Al Sharpton, of being a possible informant for the FBI with intent to provide information for money for the alleged attempted entrapment of exiled former Black Panther Assata Shakur brings to light the complex relationship between the FBI and Black Informants. It is this "Unholy Union" between the FBI and its Black Informants showing complicity in the FBI's efforts to destroy progressive Black leaders and movements with the stated objective to maintain the social order in the United States and prevent the rise of a messianic leader or group that can lead the Black masses.

Historically, this type collaborative activity has affected many Black leaders like Marcus Garvey, who ran the Universal Negro Improvement Association (UNIA) back in the early 1900s. Universal Negro Improvement Association's aim was to instill Black pride and independence from White society. At its height in the 1930s, it reached a membership high of 1,000,000. As Garvey gained more prominence, he supported anti-colonialist and socialist movements worldwide that brought him much unwelcome attention from both United States and British Intelligence officials resulting in

Black spies joining the Universal Negro Improvement Association. Emerging FBI Director J. Edgar Hoover instituted CONTELPRO- Counter Intelligence Program which was designed to stop the rise of a Black Messiah or messianic type group like the Black Panther Party. Later the aim became to survey, infiltrate, discredit, and disrupt domestic political organizations or leaders. Beloved late Supreme Court Justice Thurgood Marshall, who had the key role in the landmark legal case of Brown vs. The Board of Education, reportedly maintained a secret relationship with the FBI during the 1950s when he was a civil rights lawyer by providing information on activities within the movement especially if there was a possible "communist influence". Not unlike many other civil rights leaders, Marshall publically admonished the FBI and their tactics against Black American citizens who were being lynched along with other unconstitutional crimes committed against Blacks. Justice Marshall may have been trying to protect the National Association for the Advancement of Colored People (NAACP) from the kinds of attacks that the FBI directed against other groups by telling them that the National Association for the Advancement of Colored People were part of the fight against Communism or he may have been trying to create a relationship so they could count on more support from the FBI. Certainly, Justice Marshall was no simple informant.

Closer scrutiny into Malcolm X's life leading up to his assassination supports the theory that United States Intelligence orchestrated and coordinated his death. An FBI memorandum on March 4, 1968 among other documents shows how this government considered Malcolm X the "top" threat to the White power structure in America. This document discussed "long range" goals to prevent the rise of a messiah who could unify and electrify the militant Black Nationalist movement. Malcolm X unquestionably fit this description as previously described. In the early 1960s, United States Intelligence wrote a report on Malcolm X due to his radical influence on young Blacks, especially Black men as the National Representative of the Honorable Elijah Muhammad of the Nation of Islam.

Perhaps greater attention was paid to Malcolm as head of Temple # 7 in New York because international figures and leaders got to know Malcolm at the United Nations functions he would attend and were open to working with him beyond the confines of the Nation of Islam. Third World revolutionaries and African leaders began to take special notice of Malcolm. Once Malcolm X was forced out of the Nation of Islam and after his travels to Third World countries (where he was received as an Ambassador of Black America), the FBI would recruit Gene Roberts to join Malcolm's Organization of Afro American Unity (OAAU), modeled after Africa's Organization of African Unity (OAU).

Undercover police agent infiltrator Gene Roberts would join the Organization of Afro American Unity during its inception and rose in the group to become head of security in the group's organizational structure. Roberts worked for the New York Police Department's Bureau of Special Services (BOSS). The FBI directed Bureau of Special Services action as part of COINTELPRO against Malcolm X. As head of this hierarchy as mandated by the National Security Act of 1947, the CIA supervised the entire United States Intelligence apparatus. Another FBI agent infiltrator who joined the Nation of Islam and rose rapidly through the ranks was John X Ali, who was reportedly involved in the firebombing of Malcolm's home where his pregnant wife, Betty Shabazz, and daughters were forced out about a week before Malcolm X's assassination at the Audubon Ballroom in New York on February 21, 1965. On the day of the assassination, the FBI and police action supports the conclusion that they were heavily involved with its coordination. FBI documents suggest that John X Ali met Talmadge Hayer (aka Thomas Hagan or Mujahid Abdul Halim), who was released in 2010 after 44 years in jail, the night before the assassination.

Immediately after Malcolm X was shot, Gene Roberts was the first to arrive by Malcolm's side as seen in pictures as the one attempting to give mouth to mouth resuscitation, which is not recommended for gunshot victims hit in the chest. But Roberts revealed more in interview decades later, which supports that his real role was to check the vital signs of Malcolm to make sure he was, in fact, dead and confirmed the success of the assassins. *New York Herald Tribune* also reported that a "high profile official" confirmed that several undercover Bureau of Special Services agents were in the Ballroom audience at the assassination of Malcolm X. The evidence points to a confluence of three groups involved in Malcolm X's assassination, namely the institutional forces of NYPD, FBI and the CIA with critical informant collaboration. Gene Roberts was exposed as an undercover police agent status at a trail against the Black Panthers in 1971.

J. Edgar Hoover, Federal Bureau of Investigation Director, called the Black Panther Party, "The greatest threat to the internal security of the country," during the late 1960s and he supervised an extensive program called COINTELPRO of surveillance, infiltration, perjury, police harassment, and many other tactics designed to undermine Panther leadership, incriminate party members and drain the organization of resources and manpower. These tactics gave Hoover a hope to diminish the Black Panther Party's threat, in his mind, to the general power structure of the United States.

The Black Panther Party became an icon of the late 1960s counterculture gaining national and international prominence. The Party originally called the Black Panther Party for Self-Defense was a Black revolutionary socialist organization that operated in the United States from 1966 until around 1982 but the group's influence would be reflected in music, images and resurgent Panther-like groups like the New Panther Vanguard Movement (formerly NAAVM) out of Los Angeles. With former Black Panther Party members in the cadre, the Dallas New Black Panther Party evolved nationally to the current New Black Panther Party led by former Nation of Islam members whose progenitor was Khalid Muhammad. After Khalid's untimely death, it was led by Attorney Malik Zulu Shabazz for a while until his stepping aside to pave way for a more regional national leadership. It still reflects a "Nation of Islam Panthers" perspective.

One of the most infamous infiltration cases in the Black Panther Party was in Chicago, Illinois where William O'Neal would join the Chicago chapter of the party under the dynamic leadership of Fred Hampton. FBI Informant William O'Neal would provide information and floor plans including where Black Panther Party Illinois Chairman Fred Hampton slept in the Party house that led up to the assassination of Fred Hampton and visiting Peoria, Illinois member Mark Clark. In the early morning hours of December 4, 1969, the Chicago Police Department raided the home and immediately killed Mark Clark at the front door. Eventually, after much gun fire, they worked their way to where O'Neal indicated Chairman Fred would be, and thusly shot him multiple times in the head to insure his death. William O'Neal would be suspected of drugging

Fred that evening with tainted Kool-Aid. In 1990, O'Neal committed suicide on the Eisenhower Expressway in Chicago on Martin Luther King Day. One of the survivors of this raid was Deborah Johnson, now Akua Njeri, who was pregnant with Fred Hampton's baby and would later give birth to current activist Fred Hampton Jr.

In Los Angeles, Julio (Julius) Butler would be a key informant in the case of Elmer "Geronimo" Pratt, who was convicted of a murder on a Santa Monica tennis court in Los Angeles he did not commit when surveillance records showed he was attending a meeting in Oakland. In 1968, Carole Olson was murdered by two Black men on the Santa Monica Tennis Court. The Los Angeles Police Department had no leads until late 1970 when Black Panther Informant Julio Butler wrote to the Los Angeles Police Department that Elmer "Geronimo" Pratt (later known as Geronimo Ji-Jaga) had bragged to him about the tennis court killing. Pratt said he was innocent because the FBI had him under surveillance in Oakland when the slaying occurred in Santa Monica. Pratt was seen by the FBI as an even greater threat, not only because of his charisma, but he was also a highly trained Vietnam War veteran who taught many in the party how to fortify offices and other necessary components for survival in an attack. In 1972, the court convicted Pratt of first-degree murder while having a spy in his defense camp, which is a constitutional violation. Geronimo would serve 27 years in prison for a crime he did not commit before being released to triumphant supporters at a court house in Santa Ana, California in 1997. Geronimo Ji-Jaga died of a heart attack in Tanzania, Africa in 2011.

The Los Angeles chapter lost two of its most dynamic young leaders with the assassinations of Bunchy Carter and John Huggins at UCLA on January 17, 1969 at the hands of FBI Infiltrators, Larry and George Steiner a.k.a. the Steiner Brothers that joined the US Organization. Detective Sergeant R. Farwell recruited Donald Defreeze to work for the Public Disorder Intelligence Unit of the Criminal Conspiracy Section (CCS), whose purpose was to monitor Black political activities in California and encourage a "gang" war specifically between the Black Panthers and the US Organization. US Organization member and FBI Informant Melvin Cotton Smith helped set up arrests of Black Panthers, and when the Steiner Brothers killed Carter and Huggins, the L.A.P.D. immediately rounded up Black Panthers all over the city, but no US Organization members at the time of the killings. Following the UCLA incident, the Steiner Brothers turned themselves over to police, who had issued warrants for their arrest. They were convicted for conspiracy to commit murder and two counts of second-degree murder. The Steiner Brothers received life sentences but conveniently or with "authority" help, escaped from San Quentin Prison. George Steiner was never recaptured. After 20 years as a fugitive, Larry Steiner, who lived in Suriname, surrendered in 1994.

Panther Informant Earl Anthony wrote a detailed account of his experiences of being a FBI informant in the Black Panther Party in his book, *Spitting in the Wind*, which was very informative, albeit disappointing in the realm of what an Agent Provocateur will do to help bring down the Black Panther Party. Much can be said about our own people   working against Black progress, organizations, and individual leaders, or how they may have acted base upon some charge they were facing, jealousy, envy, the Communist issue, money, fame, or influence. In fact, they may have been the greatest traitors our race has ever seen. Not many cultures will actually turn on itself like the African-Americans in the realm of collective progress as a people unless there is the historical reality of self-hatred. Certainly in any battle, no wise general sits down with representatives of the opposition to discuss battle strategies that would make no sense. The very consequences of these collaborative actions have devastated our people. The loss of talented, sincere leaders, and groups working on our behalf has produced a "river of blood" being spilled as a direct   result   of   this   Unholy   Union.

South Africa's "Kleenex Commission"

The Truth and Reconciliation Commission (TRC) in South Africa was established to spotlight Apartheid era crimes of the minority ruled White Nationalist Party and other individual cases to be brought before a panel to have sentences upheld or amnesty being granted simply based upon telling the truth about political murders and genocidal acts. When the Commission was first established, Afrikaners or White South Africans called these panel hearings, "The Kleenex Commission" to describe the eyewitness accounts that would result in tearful, emotional moments for Black South Africans telling their stories of abuses. The Commission panel, headed at the time by Archbishop Desmond Tutu, reviewed applications and conducted hearings to determine whether amnesty would be given to the offending applicant who may have only need to be truthful about their crimes in order to be set free.

The stated objectives of this commission was organized through three committees: (1) The Human Rights Violations Committee, which investigated human rights abuses that occurred between 1960 and 1994; (2) the Reparation and Rehabilitation Committee, which was charged with restoring victims' dignity and formulated proposals to assist with rehabilitation; and (3) the Amnesty Committee, which considered applications from individuals who applied for amnesty in accordance with the provisions of the Act. While former President F.W. de Klerk appeared before the Commission and reiterated his apology for the suffering caused by Apartheid, many Blacks were angered at amnesty being granted for human rights abuses committed by the White minority government for generations. On the other side of the spectrum, former apartheid President P.W. Botha defied a subpoena to appear before the Commission, calling it a "circus". Botha's defiance resulted in a fine and suspended sentence, but these were overturned on appeal shortly thereafter. The Truth and Reconciliation Commission's emphasis on reconciliation is in sharp contrast to the approach taken by the Nuremburg Trials after World War II and other de-Nazification measures. A total of 5,392 amnesty applications were refused by the Truth and Reconciliation Commission, granting only 849 out of the 7,112 requests, including the number of additional categories such as withdrawn.

In one of the most anticipated cases, the Commission heard arguments for amnesty from the five White police officers that admitted beating to death celebrated Black leader Steve Biko, founder of the Black Conscious Movement in South Africa. When murdered, Biko was probably South Africa's best known political dissident, eclipsing even Nelson Mandela's notoriety. In death, Biko was made a martyr for young, progressive, and revolutionary Blacks, and he became another symbolic reminder of the viciousness of the Apartheid system. The five officers who admitted to interrogating and beating Steve Biko were retired Col. Harold Snyman, who led the interrogation team, Retired Lt. Col. Gideon Nieuwoudt; Ruben Marx, then a security branch warrant officer, Johan Beneke, another warrant officer, and Captain Daantjie Seibert. Steve Biko's oldest son, Nkosimathi Biko, said his family opposed amnesty being granted to the murderers of his father. Days after his arrest, Biko was naked, disoriented, and suffering from severe head injuries when he was finally driven 750 miles across South Africa for medical treatment. He died before he received any care and passed away on September 12, 1977. His case outraged the world and helped galvanize the Anti-Apartheid movement. All five were denied amnesty after years of investigation, but never admitted to being responsible for Steve Biko's death, which appalled Biko's family.

Another highly publicized case was that of Brian Mitchell, who served a 30-year sentence for the massacre of 11 women and children in 1988. Mitchell was set free after his testimony granted him amnesty, despite cries of justice from the victims' families. Lawyers for Eugene de Kock, one of Apartheid's murderous foot soldiers, presented arguments to have him granted amnesty as a Death Squad leader who admitted to terrorist bombings of anti-apartheid buildings and churches in the 1980s. De Kock spoke of dynamiting an insurgent's house in Botswana with deaf and blind children inside resulting in many deaths and injuries, and also setting fire to a building used by anti-Apartheid South Africans Bishop Conference which had old Black nuns sleeping inside, resulting in injuries. Eugene de Kock also worked with the Civilian Cooperation Bureau, an underground mercenary unit, to bomb the Community House used by an anti-apartheid coalition group called the United Democratic Front. De Kock listened to a conversation of Archbishop Tutu being terribly upset after the bombing of the Community House. De Kock later admitted before the panel that the bombing was authorized by then President P.W. Botha. The prevailing attitudes of the majority of White South Africans did not display any sympathy for these crimes committed against indigenous Black South Africans, which has been a consistent criminal settler colony position. In Steve Biko's book, *I Write What I Like*, he wrote about this prevailing attitude of White South Africans, saying, "Basically, the South African White community is a homogeneous society who enjoys a privileged position they don't deserve and, therefore, spend most of their time trying to justify what they are doing. Where difference in political position exists, they are in a position to justify their position of privilege and their usurpation of power".

Many cases remain unresolved, especially when an Act of Parliament in 1962 implemented by the White apartheid Nationalist Party that legalized imprisonment without trial. The following is a partial list of Black South Africans found dead while in police custody or detention and how these deaths were listed: September 5, 1963 – L. Ngude- suicide; September 19, 1963 – B. Merhope- no official explanation; January 24, 1964- J. Tyitya – suicide by hanging; September 9, 1964- S. Salqujie – fell seven floors; May 7, 1965 – N. Gaga – natural causes; May 8, 1965 – J. Hoye – natural cause; 1966 – J. Hamakiuayo – suicide by hanging; October 9, 1966 – H. Shonyeka – suicide; November 19, 1966 – L. Leong Pin – suicide by hanging; January 5, 1967 – A. Ah Yan – suicide by hanging; September 9, 1967 – A. Madiba – suicide by hanging; September 11, 1967 – J. Tubakwe – suicide by hanging; February 4, 1969 – N. Kgoathe – slipped in shower; February 28, 1969 – S. Modipane- slipped in shower; March 10, 1969 – J. Lenkoe – suicide by hanging; June 17, 1969 – C. Mayekiso – suicide; September 10, 1969 – J. Monaxgotia – suicide; September 27, 1969 – A. Haron- fell down stairs; January 21, 1971 – A. Timol – fell down stairs; August 5, 1976 – M. Mohapi – suicide by hanging; September 12, 1977 – Steve Biko – hunger strike; and the list goes on and on.

From a historical perspective, Black people in America can refer to similar prevailing attitudes best epitomized by the Plessy vs. Ferguson decision in 1896, which rendered that the Black man had no rights that a White man was bound to respect. The Truth and Reconciliation Commission did not attempt to address the critical issues of a radical re-distribution of the land and wealth to Black South

Africans who suffered under Apartheid, being robbed of 87% of this mineral rich land to accommodate White settlements. In 1998, a study was conducted by South Africa's Centre for the Study of Violence and Reconciliation. The Khulumani Support Group surveyed several hundred victims of human rights abuse during the Apartheid era and found that most felt that the Truth and Reconciliation Commission had failed to achieve reconciliation between the Black and White communities. In this author's opinion, "Truth without justice is injustice," and the "Kleenex Commission" would have been better served by just doing the right thing by proving that there is a consequence for any life lost, including the lives of Black South Africans.

Black Reality TV:
The Modern Minstrel Show

Shows like "Basketball Wives," "Love & Hip Hop" series, "The Real Housewives of Atlanta," "R & B Divas," "The New Atlanta," "The Gossip Game," "Married to Medicine," "Bad Girls Club," "Black Ink" and others have consistently portrayed some aspects of the African-American experience in an embarrassing light that makes the buffoonery of Amos & Andy, Stepin Fetchit and Aunt Jemima look like child's play in this modern minstrel era. I am not particularly interested in other "Reality" shows and the problems they spotlight because my first concern would be to the African-American community and its own perception of itself considering a mostly non-flattering on screen past and stereotypical portrayed present. While I do recognize that problems exist in every community, I believe that the first law of nature is self-preservation, observation, and assimilation. Our problems are best solved by our own people working together in a respectful fashion, and not acting a fool before the world, revealing all the negative perceptions others have of us, but, more importantly, the way we view ourselves.

Our dignity as a people seems to be for sale to the highest TV bidder with a "reality" star getting $5,000-$15,000 per episode, or more if it is a "celebrity" reality star of note. The most disturbing element I see on these shows are the boisterous, crazy, and violent behavior of African-American women who seem to "turn it up" when the cameras are rolling by talking about each other behind their back, cursing other women, physical altercations, and just acting a damn fool. When I think of the dignified Black women that I grew up around who displayed such poise and class that many modern Black "celebrities" can truly learn from. I am greatly disheartened by what these shows portray. Brothers on these shows are no better as they seem to portray elements of being a modern Mandingo, which will make Ken Norton's Mandingo movie portrayal look like Jaleel White's Steve Urkel considering the juggling of all these women, baby mama issues, and violent confrontations with one another.

While I agree that we as a community should be able to make light of some of our issues of deficiency, but these types of shows have taken it to a level hard to surpass. Another show which takes hypocrisy to another level is "Preachers of L.A.". This show follows the everyday lives of preachers and their families, but one is amazed at the overwhelming materialism exhibited by these "Men of the Cloth". I wonder, considering their "bling" lifestyle, if they truly refer to the Bible or Iceberg Slim's *Pimp Chronicles*. Granted, not all these shows portray African-Americans in a negative light with examples like "T.I. & Tiny: Family Hustle," "La La's Full Court Life", and "Sweetie Pies". They all depict a better and more realistic example of an African-American's perspective.

While many talented people are on some of these shows, especially the celebrities, most people you see on these shows are people we have never been seen before, and they have been elevated in the public eye to "turn up" for the viewing public. High ratings keep us riveted by each episode like a daytime soap opera. Black reality TV makes up 28% of these shows, 80% of the viewing global community watches reality TV, and 85% of the world's population watches TV. So, to have our people be so misrepresented before the world represents a modern minstrel show.

Propaganda and Programs: The Black Panther Party's Symbol with Substance _____

Revolutionary philosopher Frantz Fanon called the relationship between the classes and the masses the ExecutionerVictim Relationship. It is a relationship that has been prevalent in most of the world, especially the non-White world. The key component in building a liberation struggle is organizing the masses in direct opposition to the oppressive power structure with the primary method of propaganda and programs designed to educate and serve the people like the Survival Programs of the Black Panther Party. Propaganda without Programs is Symbol without Substance. Effective propaganda will enable the Black and oppressed community to control its own image and inform the masses to what we want and what we believe as an organizational apparatus to show the people that "our" wants are the same as "theirs".

173

The Black Panther Party's job was to inform and mobilize the community into revolutionary action. Lacking access to national radio, television or any other mass media, our people needed a communication alternative. In his autobiography, Revolutionary Suicide, Black Panther Party Co-founder Huey P. Newton wrote, "In The Black Panther (paper), the people read the true explanation of why we went to Sacramento and what happened there. We reported on events and meetings in the Black communities all over the Bay area. Until that time, the Black Panther Party had been maligned by the establishment press that was only interested in sensationalism to sell papers. But once we began to give our own interpretation of events, Black people realized how facts had been twisted by the mass media. They (community) were glad to get our point of view and the paper sold well. Our paper became a steady source of funds to help us develop our programs." The Black Panther Party Newspaper, in the late 60s and the 70s reached a circulation high of 125,000 copies per week heightening awareness and expanding programs through its sales.

The Black Panther Party was concerned specifically with the basic political aspirations, desires and social needs of the people. To see that these things were articulated in a "revolutionary fashion," through the effective use of any and all "propaganda tools" was excruciating. Properly marketed revenue generated was used to fund community based "Survival Programs" and organizing activities for the people. Platforms and Programs were essential for direction in the liberation struggle best epitomized by the Black Panthers. To justify political positions in the struggle, platforms and programs provided theory into practice. The Black Panther Party was simply an organizational mechanism to fulfill the liberation desires of Black, oppressed, and progressive people with an organizing ideological approach intended to unite all oppressed people into a political power base. This was the intent of the Black Panther Party.

Huey P. Newton and fellow co-founder Bobby Seale said in unison, "People learn basically through observation and participation. Active involvement of the people is the best consciousness raiser". In the book Seize the Time, Bobby Seale wrote, "In 1969, the Black Panther Party tried to reach millions of people, both to organize resistance to fascism and to find out about, and receive service from, the basic community programs that we have already set up and will be setting up in the future. The objective of programs set forth by revolutionaries like the Black Panther Party is to educate the masses of the people to the politics of changing the system. The politics are related to people's needs; to a hungry stomach or getting rid of the vicious pigs (cops) with their revolvers and clubs".

At the height of the Black Panther Party, its survival programs thrived in 44 cities across America, setting an example in addressing many of the basic needs of the people ranging from food, clothes, shoe giveaways, Sickle Cell Anemia testing, ambulance service (North Carolina), medical clinics, Seniors Against a Fearful Environment (the SAFE program), and other programs. The destruction of the Black Panther Party left a significant political and social "void" in the Black, oppressed and progressive community with a lack of revolutionary tradition and spirit of true love for the people. Ernesto "Che" Guervara once said, "A true revolutionary is driven by feelings of great love". The Black Panther Party served the People through Propaganda and Programs due to love for the People and knowing that the best way to reach them was to serve them – body and soul!

The Rio Games:
At the Expense of the Poor? _____

The allure of Rio de Janeiro, Zika concern along with the specter of the Olympics in 2016, provides unprecedented anticipation for this city of 6.3 million. While the citizens are excited about this grand event, what will be the effect on the Black, poor, and oppressed people in Rio, especially in the favelas that populate the rolling hills surrounding Rio de Janeiro? Brazil is unique by hosting two mega events like the World Cup and Olympics back to back, with the 2016 Olympics being a first for any South American country due to Brazil's increasing global status with economic growth and standing as a world power. But the real question is, "Are the people of Rio's favelas being displaced at the expense Olympics"? Rio has recently drawn increased attention from Amnesty International about neglect of the human rights as Rio de Janeiro carries forth large scale "urbanization" plans in anticipation for these events.

Concerns about the city government executing forced removal of partial or entire communities that exist on the bottom rung of Rio's social, economic societal level has many of these residents in direct path of developmental projects. According watchdog groups like Catalytic Communities, many poor communities like Vila Autodromo have had bulldozers present and ready to demolish homes until media was alerted and the bulldozers left. *The Rio Times* reported that in the Zona Oeste, in which Vila Autodromo is located, has been threatened many times with removal. The community is located directly across from a tract of land the City has designated for construction for the Olympics. Maniguinhos Favela and others have been evicted by the government as it prepares as host for these events and some of the neighborhoods are being demolished to build stadiums or parking lots or to enhance transportation to accommodate the droves of people coming. This has already happened to the Guimares' neighborhood, which was gutted to add lanes to a highway right behind it. Because favela houses or dwellings are built so close together, demolishing one harms the adjacent dwellings in which the occupants have not been vacated.

In 2009, the Government moved forward with its urbanization goal of urbanizing the favelas by 2020 in an effort by pacifying high profile favelas with 1,500 armed officials in complexes like Caju in Northern Rio arresting 12 drug lords. The government is on track to achieve its urbanization goal, but don't seem to have the best interests of the original residents in mind. Buyouts are being offered for residents to leave, but the amounts are not competitive and force many families to move miles away.

What feasible options are they presenting to the residents in Rio's favela residents? Money is and has always been the main motivating factor for these displacements, but as it relates to the poor and oppressed residents of the favelas, it should not be Brazil's top priority. With the Olympic effect, a report by Haddad and Haddad calculated a 4.26 multiplier that for every $1 USD invested, $3.26 will be generated until 2027 or $51.1 USD million.

The United States Department of Diplomatic Security has issued reports of Crime and Safety in Rio de Janeiro in 2013, citing that due to the Favela Pacification Program (FPP), crimes in Rio have decreased in areas of homicides in the state and city of Rio to 50% from 42 homicides per 100,000 in

2005 to 24 homicides per 100,000 in 2012. Rio resident and travel expert Lais Tammela of guideinrio.net said to me in an interview, "This program was started in 2008 with the objective of expelling the drug lords from the Rio favelas, but has its pros and cons with the lives of the residents being directly impacted more favorably". Favela Pacification Program was first introduced in November 2008, with specifically recruited and community police trained officers to enter Rio's favelas or slums to expel drugs and their armed criminal elements to establish a permanent presence called Unidade de Policia Pacificadora (UPP).

In 2012, innocent individuals, including children, were killed by balas perdidas in Rio de Janeiro with the police effectively controlling every major favela in Rio from downtown's financial district, extending south to the affluent Zona Sul (Soul Zone) and West to the Barra da Tijuca. This area includes the place where the Maracana Stadium played host to the 2014 World Cup and Barra da Tijuca being the base for the 2016 Olympic Games. The goal was for more than 10 additional pacification efforts. There have been 30 pacification operations to instill the rule of law in Rio's favelas with 8,000 newly-hired police trained to patrol these areas. Police have reasserted permanent control in dozens of previously un-pacified favelas, which are home to over a million people- a Police State.

The Pacifying Police Units or Unidade de Policia Pacificadora (UPP) is a law enforcement and "social services" program pioneered in the state of Rio de Janeiro, Brazil, which aims at reclaiming territories in the favelas that populate Rio. Implemented by State Public Security Secretary, Jose Mariano Beltrame, with the backing of Rio Governor Sergio Cabral has a stated goal of establishing 40 Unidade de Policia Pacificadora by 2014. By May 2013, 231 favelas had come under control of the Unidade de Policia Pacificadora umbrella. Brazilians were skeptical about the government's proposed urban reforms in light of the fact that the World Cup and the Olympics provided only temporary jobs, increase tourism, and influence foreign investment as the host city but not the cureall for social and economic problems that continue to hinder the country. Rio Mayor Eduardo Paes commented that Brazilian sports honchos enjoying lifetime appointments was a "scandal" and said that FIFA (Federation International Football Association) "only cares about stadiums". Once again, the interests of the Black, poor, and oppressed are swept under the Brazilian carpet to hide the dirt of the government's blind eye as the "Games of Summer" quickly approached.

My mother, Vera, me, & my sister, Mia, in

Miami – photo courtesy of Malik Ismail

Top picture – My Grandfather Jarrot Anderson Sr with me
& sister Mia – photo courtesy of Malik Ismail

Bottom picture – me and my wife Kathy in New York
City Cotton Club – photo courtesy of Malik Ismail

Top picture – Cofounders of the Black Panther Party
Bobby Seal (left) and Huey P. Newton (right) at BPP
Central Headquarters in Oakland – photo credit to It's
About Time Archives

Bottom picture – Shareef Abdullah presenting a
Panther Vanguard jacket to Nora Carter, mother of
slain L.A. BPP Leader Bunchy Carter, at the Vanguard's
Remembering the Black Panther Party Festival and
Forum – photo credit to It's About Time Archives

Montage of the Panther Vanguard Movement – photo
courtesy of Malik Ismail

PANTHER POWER
 Even Seale himself, now 61 and the surviving co-founder, has honored the new Panther Vanguard with a seven-gun salute, of sorts.
 "I think the L.A. Panthers are on target," said Seale by

volution." But as Huey, who 's chief theoretician, stated: "All tisfy the deep needs of the com-

no peace in the streets. The Re clearly demonstrated that fact. T

nnual Community Forum Festival 2,000 Bag Free Food Distribution, Nov.,

Bobby Seale's statement on the Panther Vanguard in the Pasadena Weekly other photos – picture courtesy of Malik Ismail

Left picture - me, Congresswoman Maxine Waters and Reverend Jesse Jackson speaking at a Mumia Abu Jamal rally in Los Angeles – photo credit to Kathy Robinson

Right picture – Vanguard members, including Kizzy, Goodie, & I with volunteers for a 500 free food give away to needy families in South Central L.A. – photo credit to Kathy Robinson

New Panther Vanguard Movement in formation in South Central L.A. Photo credit to The Black Panther International News Service (BPINS)

Vanguard's First Annual Festival and Forum at Marla
Gibbs Vision Theatre In Leimert Park (L.A.) –
photo credit to The Black Panther International
News Service

Vanguard Montage (2) – photo courtesy of Malik Ismail

People's Free Food Survival Program – photo credit
to The Black Panther International News Service

Top picture – Young Vanguard supporters Keyond and Chioke selling the Black Panther International News Service during Panther Vanguard's Busing to Prison program – photo credit to The Black Panther International News Service

Bottom picture – montage of New Panther Vanguard Movement newspapers including The Black Panther International News Service –photo courtesy of Malik Ismail

Weekly English language class for Spanish spe
International Panther headquarters.

Children's Saturday Education program at the International
Panther headquarters.

Programs, classes and community forums at the
Vanguard's International Panther Headquarters in L.A. –
photo credit to The Black Panther International News
Service

Top picture – Former L.A. BPP member Elder Ronald Freeman, a mentor to Vanguard members –photo credit to·It's About Time Archives

Bottom picture – Vanguard and former L.A. BPP member Shareef Abdullah and former L.A. BPP member Wayne Pharr, also another mentor to Vanguard members – photo credit to The Black Panther International News Service

Top left picture – me and Stokely Carmichael (Kwame Ture) in Ghana–photo courtesy of Malik Ismail

Top right picture–me meeting with Khoisan X, Secretary General of the Pan Africanist Congress, in Johannesburg, South Africa – photo credit to Kathy Robinson

Bottom left picture – me and Elizabeth Sibeko in Soweto –photo credit to Kathy Robinson

Bottom right picture – me and David DuBois, stepson of W.E.B. DuBois, in Accra, Ghana–photo courtesy of Malik Ismail

Top picture Boko, unnamed sister, Kwaku Duren and Sister Pat at Vanguard's 2nd Annual Forum Festival at Compton College where 2,000 bags of free grocery was given to needy families – photo credit to It's About Time Archives

Bottom picture – Panther Vanguard comrades in Oakland for the 30th Anniversary of the BPP in 1996 – photo credit to It's About Time Archives

Top Left picture – me and Kathleen Cleaver – photo credit to Kathy Robinson

Right picture – me and Bobby Seale at D.C. BPP Reunion – photo credit to Kathy Robinson

Bottom Left picture – me and Elaine Brown – photo credit to Kathy Robinson

The Panthers' new pa[t]

Ex-militants now involved in community

By SHANTE MORGAN
Copley News Service

San Diego Tribune feature on the Vanguard with Hanif Mack, Kwaku Duren and me – photo credit to Copley News Service /San Diego Tribune

Top Left picture—me, Kamau Osiris, Fred Hampton Jr and Akua Njeri in Chicago —photo credit to Logan Bossier

Top Right picture — Kwaku, me, and Boko at D.C .BPP Reunion — photo credit to It's About Time Archives

Bottom picture — Kwaku speaking at L.A .Ciy Hall rally with Zahkee and other Vanguard members —photo credit to The Black Panther International News Service

Top Left picture – Unity in the Community Free BBQ Rally flyer – photo courtesy of Malik Ismail

Right picture – NPVM's Free Health Screening program flyer – photo credit to The Black Panther International News Service

Bottom Left – Panther Vanguard's Dreamer Black and Vanguard supporter Peace Punk at Headquarters (L.A.) – photo credit to The Black Panther International News Service

Top picture – Billy X Jennings of It's About Time BPP Commemorative Committee –photo credit to It's About Time Archives

Bottom picture – Participants, including Bobby Seale, at Washington D.C. BPP Reunion & Conference –photo credit to It's About Time Archives

Vanguard Montage – photo courtesy of Malik Ismail

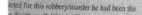

Top picture – cover of the Vanguard's The Black Panther International News Service covering Geronimo JiJaga (Pratt) release from prison after almost 28 years as a political prisoner

Bottom picture – picture I took of Geronimo headed outside of prison – photo courtesy of Malik Ismail

Chairman Fred mural with Mensah Chiraq Sojah, Fred
Hampton Jr, Kamau Osiris, me, and Loretta Dillon in
Chicago – photo credit to Logan Bossier

"Our goal in life is to discover our gift, our purpose in life is to give it away" –

Pablo Picasso

American Renaissance Man: Paul Robeson

By Rolling Out | February 7, 2014

Wife Essie, Paul, and Paul Jr at Enfield, Connecticut home - 1941

(Photo provided by Malik Ismail)

There has been no greater omission from our historical past than the name of Paul Robeson, who has been seemingly written out of American history as an African American icon reserved for the likes of Malcolm X, Martin Luther King Jr, Harriet Tubman, Adam Clayton Powell Jr., Frederick Douglass, Sidney Poitier, Muhammad Ali, Marian Anderson and others in various fields of excellence as the least known figure in our history. America's deletion of Robeson in this country's history shows the power of the United States government's ability to erase an individual from our national consciousness. Robeson was scorned in his own country, yet beloved as a global superstar and perhaps the greatest American Renaissance man of the 20th century as an athlete, scholar, lawyer, singer, activist, film director, actor, orator, musicologist, labor force supporter, concert singer, historian and global citizen. Born on April 9, 1898, in Princeton, N.J., as the youngest of three brothers Reeve, William Drew Jr, Benjamin and sister Marian to his parents Rev. William Drew Robeson, a former escaped slave, and Maria Louisa Robeson, who would die tragically in a house fire when Paul was 6 years old.

After high school Paul earned a scholarship to Rutgers University in New Jersey, one of three blacks in school's history, where he would become an honor student, a two time All-American football star, play basketball, baseball and run track. At Rutgers, he was an academic genius graduating Phi Beta Kappa and becoming Valedictorian of his graduating class at school where he was affectionately called "Robeson of Rutgers." After graduating from Rutgers, he would attend the prestigious Columbia Law School where he would become the third black graduate in that institution's history. Paul married Eslanda Goode after meeting in New York, who would bear him a son named Paul Robeson Jr. After becoming disenchanted with the law field in New York because of the racism he encountered and encouraged by Essie, he decided

leave the law practice to use his talents as a singer and actor soon to become the most significant Black actor in America on stage and the silver screen. Paul was the first black actor who rose to international prominence in film, bringing dignity and respect to Black characters. He was the actor who gave the memorable performance and profound interpretation of Shakespeare's Othello in modern times. Paul became one of America's greatest concert and interpretive artists and the first, along with Roland Hayes, to raise Black spirituals to their rightful place of dignity in the best concert halls throughout in the world. He was an accomplished musicologist and symbol of excellence on the American stage scene. Paul also used his singing talents as an activist and spokesman for the Black, poor and oppressed in America and throughout the world becoming an inspiration to the American Labor Movement.

Lena Horne and Paul war – bond campaign – 1942
(Photo provided by Malik Ismail)

Paul Robeson was a brilliant scholar of language and world culture, recognized by some of the world's most respected historians; he also studied, spoke and wrote more than 20 languages, including many African languages, Chinese, Russian and Arabic as a linguist. He would be embraced as a global icon wherever he went, but his support of liberation movements in Africa in the 30s and 40s, friendship with Soviet Premier Nikita Khrushchev and the Russian people would cause his persecution in the U.S. during the "Cold War" era.

In the 1950s, the entire country was swept up in the antiCommunist hysteria led by U.S. Senator Joseph McCarthy of Wisconsin, figurehead of McCarthyism, who wanted to identify individuals with Communist ties and Paul became an easy target for his outspoken ideas. He was prevented from working abroad with his passport being held for 8 years which would curtail a brilliant career at that point. Paul testified before an Anti-Communism Committee for Un-American activities where he told them in essence, that whatever party he belonged to and who his global friends were was nobody's business but his own. Even black baseball pioneer Jackie Robinson testified against Paul due to some statements made by Robeson in Paris and very few black celebrities stood by him at this time except Lena Horne and a handful of supporters.

Though he became a victim of McCarthyism and his own integrity, he incredibly survived when that era ended to resume his career as an artist in America and abroad. Old age, illness and the death of his beloved Essie in 1965 finally dictated his retirement from public life after more than four decades in the spotlight. He died in Philadelphia where he lived with his sister Marian on January 23, 1976 at the age of 77 as virtually a recluse with little public acknowledgement of his great accomplishments. Paul Robeson should always remembered for his activism for his people and the poor working class people around the world along with his brilliant stage career, his being a global goodwill ambassador, singer, film director, actor in great films like the classic Emperor Jones, King Solomon's Mines, The Song of Freedom, Sanders of the River, The Proud Valley and many other films. The Paul Robeson story should indeed be a part of school curriculums in elementary schools, high schools and colleges throughout the country. As a people, we need to rediscover this great man and not allow his memory to be lost in history.

Black Leadership: Soldiers or Sellouts?

By **Rolling Out** | March 19, 2014

Editor's note: The following op-ed has not been edited and the opinions expressed are solely those of the writer.

Our people tend to rally behind charismatic leaders, exalting them with our moral and financial support. African Americans have supported leaders promising to get us to the "Promised Land" but they themselves are usually the only one to arrive at this desirable destination. Unfortunately, a profitable enterprise can be made out of a people's suffering, political aspirations, hopes and desires. Black leadership is big business for individuals inspired by money and prestige based off our struggle as a people. Our people's yearning for freedom has often been stifled by leadership that has sold out the struggle. Paid black leadership has been around a long time. Many of these "socalled" leaders have used their visibility and social positions as a means to receiving "token" support from the masses of Black folk. These kinds of leaders compromise the destiny of their own people for cold cash. Slavery was and is the bedrock of the Western World capitalist economy.

Too many of our "leaders" have gotten used to the limousines, mansions, entourages and platinum credit cards, financed by our people's desire to be free. Often times this kind of leader fights "in words" rather than "in deeds", which in this author's opinion makes them nothing more than "cheerleaders" who might as well be wearing pompons and a hula skirt. As a historically oppressed people in America, we cannot afford to have leaders who get caught up in the financial gain off the struggle of our people. Many "leaders" tell our people to "continue the struggle" but never talk about achieving "victory" or established time tables for achievement. Is it because they are being "paid" as a direct result of the struggle? Paid black leadership generally doesn't want to "lead" our struggle, the want to "contain" our struggle acting as a "buffer" between the Black masses and the oppressive power structure. The "paid" leader will stand between his people and the system but never really wanting them as a mass to go after the power structure. They will criticize the government but never seriously engage it or demand fundamental changes that will after the masses of Black folk.

Take the 1963 March on Washington as a historical example. As Malcolm X pointed out, "the masses were the ones talking about marching on Washington, D.C. to shut down the city's functioning." When the Power Structure was advised of this "steamroller" coming, they called all the prominent Civil Rights leaders to the Carlisle Hotel in New York to meet with Robert Kennedy, then Attorney General under his brother President John Kennedy's administration. At this meeting were Dr. Martin Luther King Jr, Roy Wilkins, Whitney Young, A. Philip Randolph, James Foreman and John Lewis who would be called the "Big Six" of the major Civil Rights organizations. Money, constituents and influence always plays a part when it comes to "paid leaders" seeking prominence in the Black community as their "voice". Robert Kennedy and Steven Corrier set up the Council for United Civil Rights Leadership for fund-raising and catapulted the "Big Six" to lead it when they were not originally in the march as Malcolm X articulated in his famous "Message to the Grassroots speech" This council was co-chaired by Whitney Young of the Urban League and Steven Corrier of the Kennedy Administration. Reportedly, the Kennedy Administration gave the "Big Six" $800,000 prior to this "March" and $ 700,000 after its conclusion totaling a million and a half dollars split up between their respective Civil Rights organizations. Not suggesting that the "Big Six" were money hungry, but it is a fact that the original intent of the March was more militant but what developed was more like a picnic and if you are financially supported by the very system of government that you were marching on the end goals cannot be expected to be the same.

This era's "leaders" like Rev. Jesse Jackson, Rev. Al Sharpton, Minister Louis Farrakhan, Dr. Cornell West, Tavis Smiley and many others have done some good things to spotlight problems that plague the African-American community but usually for a fee or honorarium. During the Black Power era in the 60s and 70s there was more of a grassroots local organizing effort amongst the leadership which would produce a Black Panther Party in the Revolutionary Nationalist perspective along with The Republic of New Africa (RNA) providing a more land focused Black Nationalist view point and of course the long standing Nation of Islam from the Spiritual Nationalist perspective which has always had a great impact on the local brother and sister on "The Block". The Platform and Program perspective on the local level which could inspire a national program seemed to transcend the more prominent leaders' objective to be in the news and the media's darlings.

Malcolm X once said, "No individual should rise above the condition of his people" which meant to be a deterrent to socalled leaders who used their notoriety and "fame" to make money but do little to nothing in the community. Active involvement of the community is the best conscious raiser in pursuit of the fundamental change the people need by working on and implementing each step of the Platform and Program which offered the best method of complete constructive change which can be called a revolution. Indeed fundraising to support organizations is a vital component for any organization but with "Leaders" getting speaking fees or honorariums, it is hopeful that the money filters down to some program that directly serves the needs of the community. According to Goviva Speaking Bureau, speaking fees for Jessie Jackson range from $50,000 to $100,000, Minister Louis Farrakhan's range is from 35,000 to $50,000 which is comparable to what Rev. Al Sharpton makes for appearances. T.D. Jakes and others also command a sizable contribution in the religious evangelist arena, so this can be big business around a cult personality and if money is not used correctly the community they claim to serve is the biggest loser.

Brazil: A Taste of Africa

By **Rolling Out** | August 24, 2013

As I boarded the plane for my first trip to Brazil, I did not harbor any delusions of grandeur about the culture I would discover – at the world famous Copacabana Beach, the iconic Christ –The Redeemer Statue, Favela's in the hills of Rio or a sighting of the fictional "Girl from Ipanema." What I did expect was to find a "Taste of Africa" in the wonderful cities of both Rio de Janeiro and Salvador Bahia.

I traveled to Brazil mainly to attend Carnival: the world famous celebration that people from all over the world attend in the month of February, but I was delighted to discover that much of the character of the places I visited had an overwhelming and obvious African influence through the makeup of the population, food, culture and customs of this distinctly tribal environment. Prior to traveling to Brazil, I learned that outside of Africa, Brazil has the largest population of people of African descent in the world. As of 2007, the Brazilian metropolitan area with the largest percentage of blacks is Salvador Bahia at 62% and Rio having a lesser but sizable Black population. Over nearly three centuries, from the late 1500s to the 1860s, Brazil was consistently the main destination for enslaved Africans in the Americas.

In 1888, Brazil abolished slavery but had the largest population of African and "creole" people in any one colony in the Western Hemisphere. These statistics were not shocking to me but a bit surprising even with the knowledge that most Africans that were stolen from Africa were brought to Brazil in particular and South America in general due to the shorter voyage as opposed to America, Central America or the Caribbean. I was 18 years old when I first dreamed of traveling to Brazil but of course as time and interests changed over the years, I was delayed. Africa became my central place of interest. I've traveled to Ghana, Egypt and South Africa multiple times.

The first day, I arrived in the Barra da Tijuca area of Rio, which is not as congested as the Copacabana or Ipanema Beach areas that are more popular for tourists. After my 9hour flight from Miami, I mustered enough energy to walk along the boardwalk where I heard the beating of drums throughout the beach areas, which for native Rio residents or Cariocas, is a weekend pilgrimage as thousands of residents descend upon all the beaches of Rio.

I was literally guided by the tribal rhythm as I made my afternoon stroll and enjoyed the spontaneous "parties" that would have people dancing to the beat miles up the coastline. Brazilians seem to emphasize their national pride in being Brazilian than their ethnic pride due to race but, of course, the stark reality of the majority of Blacks living in the Favelas that are situated in the rolling hills of Rio de Janeiro which I had the opportunity to visit the Famous "City of God" or Cidade de Deus and the largest Favela called Rocinha in Rio's south zone. I found so many Afro-Brazilians to be friendly and curious to my presence and interaction with them. It was like finding lost family members that were unfamiliar in language and custom but united in the global recognition of being Black. The food was connected to Africa, like this dish called "Moqueca" – a fish, beef or shrimp stew made with Dende' or Palm Oil, a direct connection to Africa.

The Carnival in Rio was amazing and after my stay in Rio ended, I caught a plane to Salvador Bahia and saw where the African influence is the strongest in all of Brazil. Being in Salvador Bahia was like getting off a plane and going any large Black urban area I have ever been to in the United States with so many Brothers and Sisters in the city. Seeing many of the Sisters in the white traditional dresses and smoking cigars, an indication to adherence to the African connected Santeria Religion, as well as visiting the historic areas like Pelourinho Historic District in the seaport area of the colonial district. I also was amazed that an airport in Bahia was named after a Black Man named Zumbi who led a slave revolt against the Portuguese and his statues are viewed prominently throughout Bahia .What an experience to get a Taste of Africa thousands of miles from Africa, yet very near to my surprise.

Bahia

Cuba: Behind the Palm Curtain

By Rolling Out | November 30, 2013

The Soviet Union was commonly called the "Iron Curtain" back during the height of the Cold War, so certainly Cuba can be thusly called the "Palm Curtain" due to its forbidden fruit image, tropical allure and Communist perspective on this island of 11 million people. The capital of Cuba is Havana and the second largest city is Santiago de Cuba in this country struggling for redevelopment after America's infamous embargo and the fall of the Soviet Union, yet it has both a high life expectancy and literacy rate even as it is considered a developing country. As I arrived at Jose Marti International Airport in Havana Cuba, thoughts of how this Island was such a pivotal place in world history, one feels as though they have stepped back in time as I ride toward my hotel in one of these classic cars as my skillful driver maneuvers this drop top 57 Chevy in a parade of other classic cars navigating congested Havana. Cuba's diversity is reflected in the faces of those as I pass the iconic Revolutionary Square, where the Jose' Marti' Monument resides and the place where Fidel and Raul Castro would speak for hours to millions facing another iconic image reflected by the face of Argentinian Ernesto Che' Guevara on a building nearby, who remains a lasting hero of the Cuban Revolution.

In 1959, Castro and his band of revolutionaries inspired by their July 26 Movement that marked the first attempt by Castro to overthrow the government of Fulgencio Batista, he would meet Che' and others exiled in Mexico to depart there for a journey that would change the course of world history with the Cuban Missile Crisis in October 1962, that literally brought the world to the edge of a nuclear war. Historically, Cuba under Castro was a major contributor to anti-imperialist wars in Africa, Central America and Asia. Castro sent tens of thousands of troops to Angola when Apartied South Africa was invading Angola. Historically, Cuba is the only minor developing country to have projected influence on the world stage that has a characteristic of a major global power.

Present Cuba is contrast with some revamped hotels and classic cars that remain relics of days of old and the current infrastructure has very little importation of new products. The population of Cuba has very complex origins and intermarriage between diverse groups is general. The Institute for Cuban and Cuban-American Studies at the University of Miami say that 62% is Black which is interesting. The Cuban people are known to be friendly and courteous but one is taken by surprise to learn the most popular foreigner that Cubans take great interest in is Americans.

Around Havana, one notices many monuments to The Revolution in 1959 but very little images of Fidel and Raul Castro only Che Guevara and Camilo Cienfuegos who remain martyrs with Che being assassinated October 9, 1967 in Bolivia and Camilo dying in a plane crash October 28, 1959 shortly after the Revolution. There is a monument to Afro Cuban hero Antonio Maceo, who was a key figure in the war of independence against Spain and was commonly called, "The Bronze Titan" as an almost a mythical icon on the level of Jose' Marti', the central person in opposition to Spain's colonization of the island and iconic hero of Fidel Castro.

Between me getting rest at Hotel National, where Nat King Cole, Frank Sinatra, Ava Gardner and many others graced its hallways, I loved seeing Old Havana which has a historic colonial splendor about it with the old buildings, plaza, cobblestone walkways and those wonderful Afro Cuban sisters wearing colorful decorative dresses, smoking those Cuban cigars, certainly I helped myself to a few during my visit. In Cuba, along with other parts of the Caribbean and South America, the Santeria

Religion is very popular. This religion is considered a syncretic Yoruba based religion of West Africa with elements of voodoo, Roman Catholicism and Christian nomenclature. Cuba is official a secular state and religious freedoms increased during the 1980s. Cuban culture is influenced by its melting pot of cultures, primarily those of Africa and Spain. Cuban music is very rich and is the most commonly known expression of culture.

The cuisine of Cuba is a fusion of Spanish, African and Caribbean influences. Though the US embargo has affected all Cubans, the free health care, education and overall literacy programs instituted by the Castro government seemingly has made Cuba a highly literate, healthy society. Despite tremendous economic hardships, Cuba does seem to be making a great effort to equalize opportunity for all which has been the lasting testament to the Revolution- behind the Palm Curtain.

Egypt: Land of Antiquities

By Rolling Out | March 27, 2014

I have been very fortunate to have visited Egypt on four occasions but each time I travel to this land of historical antiquities, I remain overwhelmed by the wondrous monuments and history of this North African country. The monuments in Egypt have been consistently described as one of the great "Wonders of the World" as lasting testaments of time going back 10,000-15,000 years ago. From the pyramids of Giza, to historic Cairo, the north flowing Nile River, wonderful bazaars, mosques, temples and historical splendor in this country of 84 million people, you remain in awe of this land. Egypt is a transcontinental country being one of the most populous in all of Africa, the Middle East and the 15th most populated in the world. About half of Egypt's residents live in urban areas, with most spread across the densely populated centers of greater

Cairo, Alexandria and other major cities in the Nile Delta. Depending on the political climate in Egypt at time of travel, choose a time of great stability to travel there.

The economy of Egypt is one the most diversified in Africa and the Middle East with the sectors such as tourism, agriculture, industry and service at almost equal levels. Egypt is also considered to be a regional and middle power with significant cultural, political and military influence in North Africa, the Middle East and the Muslim world. This Nile Valley civilization begins with the great Nile River itself which is believed to be the longest river in the world at 4,145 miles. As you arrive in Cairo, the obvious realization that you are in a military country is evident as you deplane with armed soldiers near each plane that lands. As you are being taken to your hotel the constant sound of horns resonates in your eardrum. One finds a dramatic contrast in the city because there will be modern hotel with luxury cars in front but a ways down the street you will see an old concrete hut with a person riding a donkey driven cart filled with hay.

The Great Sphinx at Giza

Cairo is a contrast of eras in this modern time, depending where you are in the city, you can appear to be in another century. Cairo is the largest city on the African continent, nicknamed "The City of a Thousand Minarets," where one can visit Giza to see the three Great Pyramids and the Sphinx of King Khafra (4th dynasty), the Mosque of Mohammed Ali where Malcolm X had his picture taken while praying and touring in 1964, the famous market bazaars in Cairo where centuries earlier Mali King Mansa Musa brought a caravan of 10,000 and actually flooded the gold market in Cairo in route to Mecca for Hajj or Pilgrimage and the wonderful

227

Museum of Cairo where many artifacts are on display including the bust of Imhotep, who was the worlds earliest architect, engineer and physician in the 27th century B.C.

As one leaves Cairo to travel further South to see Luxor (Thebes) called, "The City of a Hundred Gates", a two hour flight of Cairo, where one will be amazed to see the temples and the Egyptian center of power. The Temples of Karnak, the Valley of the Kings where tombs of Rames, Tutankhamen, Queen Hatshepsut, Queen Nefertiti and others can be seen there as well. Also, going even further South, one can visit the grand Temple of Abu Simbel with the four sitting Kings outside the temple. Though Egypt has an ethnically diverse population now, according to scholars like Historian Chancellor Williams, the Black African roots to what is known as Egypt is clear. By Williams' account, there was no "Egypt" before the Black king from whose name it was indirectly derived. Before that the country was called Chem (Khem) or Chemi (Khemi) — another name indicating its black inhabitants because they referred to their land as Kemet which means the "Black Land" or Kemmiu, which translates as "the blacks." Chemistry is believed to be the earliest science of the Chemi (Khemi or Kemite) people of Kemet — a black science. Many white scholars try to suggest it referred to the black soil of Egypt, not the people but personally I have traveled all over Egypt or Kemet and did not see the black soil in question.

When considering that Nile Valley civilization, which includes the Sudan and Ethiopia, the contribution to the civilization around the world, including Europe, Greece, Spain and other lands, its contribution is incredible. The parent of what would later be called Egyptian Civilization came from the South (Upper Egypt) where there are more pyramids than in the North (Lower Egypt) so in essence, it's culture began in the south where you have Sudan, Nubia and Upper Egypt spreading the culture up the north-running Nile River. The land of Egypt or Kemet continues to amaze the world as one of the great wonders of the world in this land of antiquities.

Fannie Lou Hamer, An Unsung Civil Rights Era Heroine

By Rolling Out | February 1, 2015

Fanny Lou Hamer, a leader of the Freedom Democratic Party, speaks before the credentials committee of the Democratic national convention in Atlantic City, August 22, 1964, in efforts to win accreditation for the group as Mississippi's delegation to the convention. The Freedom group, composed almost entirely of Negroes, is opposed by the regular all – white Mississippi delegation. (AP Photo/stf)

Fannie Lou Hamer's legacy is more profound than what's come to be known as the Civil Rights Movement catch phrase: "I'm sick and tired of being sick and tired."

Perhaps the most underappreciated, least celebrated political figure in the pantheon of civil rights was American voting rights and civil rights leader Fannie Lou Hamer, a truly unsung hero. Fannie was the central figure in the Mississippi Freedom Democratic Party and was catapulted to national prominence during the 1964 Democratic National Convention in Atlantic City, New Jersey. Hamer's Mississippi grassroots, plain speaking manner and fervent commitment to be a voice for her people would be on display for the world to see as she articulated the feelings of Southern Blacks trying to exercise their constitutional right to vote and run in political electoral arenas. Her passionate speeches inspired and electrified the National Democratic Convention which touched the hearts of blacks and progressive whites as she talked about the plight of Southern Blacks under the restrictive, unconstitutional methods "Jim Crow" Mississippi would use to deny Blacks the right to vote.

Fannie Lou Hamer (birth name Fannie Lou Townsend) was born on Oct. 6, 1917, in Montgomery County, Mississippi, as the youngest of 20 children to sharecropper parents, Ella and James Townsend. The Townsends' income depended upon the harvested crops they would gather for the landowner, who in turn would pay a small amount for their share during harvest. At age 6, Hamer was weeding (clearing or removing weeds) the cotton fields then helped pick the cotton. Hamer went to school up until the eighth grade, a lot more schooling in a plantation economy than most black children opportunity to attend at that time. Fannie Lou Townsend married Perry "Pap" Hamer in 1944 and they settled on the Marlow plantation as sharecroppers outside Ruleville, Mississippi.

Hamer, a plantation records keeper, could read and write very well, which impressed many. The Hamers did not have any children of their own but raised two girls that came from two different impoverished homes and later adopted the two daughters of one of the girls who died. Hamer had deeply religious beliefs and was someone many came to for help with disputes. When young civil rights workers arrived in Ruleville in the Mississippi Delta in 1962, they were looking for local Blacks to help register Black voters amid the White hostility that could result in harassment, violence or death. It was there that these civil rights workers found 44-year-old Hamer. In turn, Hamer was attracted to these young activists, especially those in the Student Non-Violent Coordinating Committee, where another middle-aged committed woman named Ella Baker would help establish the organization. Baker is commonly regarded as the "Godmother of SNCC."

Hamer's courage and tenacity came to the attention of SNCC chief organizer Bob Moses, who would train many Freedom Riders to descend upon the South and the challenging Mississippi Delta. Hamer became a SNCC field secretary in early 1963. Months later, Fannie attended a citizenship training school sponsored by the Martin Luther King Jr lead Southern Christian Leadership Conference in

Charleston, South Carolina, to learn how to instruct her neighbors about the benefits of citizenship and their right to vote as citizens. Hamer lost her job as a timekeeper, where she worked for 18 years because of these organizing activities.

Hamer remained committed to the civil rights voting cause and the young organizers who brought her into the struggle. Hamer was quoted as saying, "they treated us like we was special and we loved 'em and trusted 'em." Hamer would dedicate the rest of her life to the Civil Rights Movement on the regional and national level. Civil and voting rights became her calling and mission. During this time in Mississippi, state voter registration requirements had a person who would determine and interpret a randomly selected section of the state constitution which was a complicated stipulation. Prospective Black voters inevitably failed the test, whether well-educated or not, often by a White person who would not pass legalized voter criteria themselves without the road block set up for Blacks. By the spring of 1965, after years of voting efforts by Blacks in Sunflower County, only 155 black people were registered to vote, which represented only 1.1 percent of those eligible to vote, while more than 7,000 Whites were registered, which amounted to around 80 percent of Whites who were eligible to vote.

During the "Freedom Summer" of 1964, the Mississippi Freedom Democratic Party or "Freedom Democrats" was organized with the purpose of challenging Mississippi's allWhite delegation that ignored the democratic rights of black residents to have a hand in the political process that all Mississippians were afforded, not representative of the state's constituency. Hamer was elected vice-chair and Aaron Henry, a longtime NAACP activist, headed the group. The Mississippi Freedom Democratic Party would descend upon Atlantic City, New Jersey, where the 1964 Democratic National Convention would take place. Prior to this effort, Blacks in Mississippi tried to participate in selecting delegates who would nominate the party's presidential candidate, but they were turned away.

Actor and activist Harry Belafonte, who would often appear with Hamer at movement events in the South, said that Hamer's voice was so inspirational and "from the heart would bring another dimension." The Freedom Democrats efforts drew national attention to blacks in Mississippi and the entire South and challenged then-President Lydon B. Johnson seeking re-election. Johnson could have conceivably lost states electoral votes because Southern delegates were leaning toward Barry Goldwater — Johnson's Republican challenger. Hamer drew a great deal of attention from the media, which angered Johnson who he referred to Hamer as "that loud illiterate woman." Hamer was invited to address the convention's Credentials Committee where she articulated the problems she and other Blacks had trying to register to vote. One of Hamer's poignant and dramatic moments during her testimony was her statement, "All of this is on account we want to register, to become first-class citizens, and if the Freedom Democratic Party is not seated now, I question America. Is this America? Land of the free and the home of the brave, where we have to sleep with our phones off the hooks because our lives are threatened daily because we want to live as decent human beings. Is this America?"

At the White House, President Johnson called an emergency press conference in an effort to divert press coverage away from Hamer's testimony, however many television networks ran her speech late at night and the Credentials Committee received thousands of calls and letters in support of the Freedom Democrats. Hamer's dramatic testimony would lead to a compromise involving President Johnson, Sen. Hubert Humphrey, Walter Mondale, Walter Reuther and J. Edgar Hoover. The Democratic Party later adopted a clause which demanded equality of representation from their state's delegations in 1968 that recognized the rights of all. Hamer continued her work in Mississippi for the Freedom Democrats and for local civil rights causes. She ran for Congress in 1964 and 1965 and was seated as a member of Mississippi's official delegation to the Democratic National Convention of 1968 where she spoke out against the Vietnam War. Fannie Lou Hamer died of heart failure from hypertension on March 14, 1977, in Mound Bayou, Mississippi, at the age of 59 years old and she is buried in her hometown of Ruleville. On Hamer's tombstone is engraved one her most famous quote, "I'm sick and tired of being sick and tired." On the Mount Rushmore of civil rights leaders, she was indeed an unsung hero.

Ghana: Black Shining Star

By Rolling Out | December 28, 2013

The Republic of Ghana celebrated its 50th year of independence from colonial rule on March 6, 2007. This former British colony gained its independence on March 6, 1957, as newly elected President Osageyfo Kwame Nkrumah announced before the world, " Today, we are free" as millions of his countryman spilled into the streets to celebrate this West African nation becoming the first sub-

Saharan African country to achieve independence from colonial rule. In 1950, Nkrumah was jailed for his political organizing as head of the radical Convention People's Party. However, when the colonial government was pressured to hold democratic elections, the C.P.P. swept into power. Kwame Nkrumah went from prisoner to Head of State and was escorted to C.P.P. headquarters directly from jail as thousands lined the streets.

On the eve of Independence in 1957, many crowded into Black Star Square Arena in Accra, Ghana, to witness this historic ceremony marking the end of colonial rule. It was exactly 12 midnight on March 6, 1957, when the British flag was taken down and one minute later, the new flag of Ghana was raised in its place. The colors on the new flag of Ghana were the Pan Africanist colors of red, yellow and green in horizontal formation with a Black Star in the middle which represents the respect Kwame Nkrumah had for Pan Africanist Marcus Garvey and his Black Star Ship line to carry Blacks in the Diaspora back home to Africa. As head of the Universal Negro Improvement Association, Garvey created this steamship line for that specific task (One week before departure of this ship, it was sabotaged and sank in New York harbor where it rest today). President Nkrumah, a Pan Africanist himself, was always quoted as saying the "Black Star in the flag is a guiding light for those Africans in the Diaspora to come home," fulfilling the Pan African vision of Marcus Garvey, George Padmore, Sekou Ture' and W.E.B. Du Bois. In the spirit of this vision, Nkrumah asked W.E.B. DuBois to come live in Ghana after being railroaded by racist America. DuBois, in a final act of refute, renounced his American citizenship to settle permanently in Ghana where he died on Aug. 28, 1963, the same day as the March on Washington led by Dr. Martin Luther King Jr. The body of W.E.B. DuBois was laid to rest at his residence in Accra, Ghana which is now the W.E.B. DuBois Center for Pan African Culture.

Kwame Nkrumah had a "revolutionary vision" of not just Ghana becoming a great nation but a greater vision of the United States of Africa being established, which was not a popular idea with Africa's colonial masters at the time. Despite Nkrumah's vision, he would be overthrown by a military coup while on a diplomatic trip to China and would live the remainder of his remarkable life with his friend Guinea President Sekou Ture' who would name Nkrumah copresident of Guinea, West Africa despite his reluctance to accept a gracious act from his lifelong friend. Democratic rule has proven to be better than coup after coup, which robbed Africa of brilliant minds that could have found common political ground through democracy. The year 1997 marked a new day in African politics when Flight Lt. Jerry John Rawlings was re-elected to his second term in widely held democratic elections and after fulfilling his term, paved way for a succession of democratically elected leaders John Kufuor, John Atta Mills and current President John Dramani Mahama. Un-acknowledged in Europe and the U.S., Ghana has proven to be the most politically stable sub-Saharan African country to this very day. Blessed with a stable and peaceful government, Ghana's economy is steadily expanding, wonderful host attractions, excellent hotels and new convention facilities such as the Accra International Conference Center — plus Africa's friendliest, most hospitable people means that tourism and "repatriation" is set to grow significantly in the 21st century.

Geographically, this tropical West African nation, formerly called the Gold Coast, is bound on the north and northwest by Burkina Faso, on the east by Togo, on the south by the Atlantic Ocean and on the west by Cote' d'Ivoire. The name Ghana was taken from the highly developed and sophisticated Ghana Empire which flourished in West Africa between the 4th and 10th century A.D. Ghana is about the same size of the United Kingdom, with a population of over 17 million. The economy is founded in agriculture, producing cocoa, high quality indigenous shea butter, mining (gold, diamonds, manganese, timber) and hydroelectric power from the Akosombo Dam providing diversification. Even TV host Anthony Bourdain of No Reservations did a show from Ghana and learned that Ghana and African Americans share a special relationship as described by then Ghana's Minister of Tourism and Diaspora Affairs Jake Obetsebi-Lamptey, with the largest concentration of African Americans settling in Ghana more than anywhere else on the African continent — among the famous are, of course, W.E.B. DuBois and Maya Angelou who lived there for a while. In 1994, The Nation of Islam hosted an

International Saviors Day Convention that drew 2,000 blacks from the diaspora in one of the largest "pilgrimages" in the 20th century, and this writer was among the participants. This convention culminated with Minister Louis Farrakhan addressing 30,000 at Black Star Arena.

"AKWABAA," means welcome and it is the word Ghanaians use to greet visitors arriving in Ghana. For blacks in the diaspora, this "pilgrimage" is not complete until they visit the "slave dungeons" along the coastal region of Ghana, Cape Coast and Elmina specifically. Visitors light candles inside these dark fortresses as they make their way to the infamous "Door of No Return," where many would depart Africa never to return and have generations of their descendants to live and die in foreign lands either in Europe, South America, the Caribbean or America. Men and women were separated by sex and they waited sometimes months in sweltering castle heat, before leaving their homeland forever. At the Cape Coast Dungeon, there is a large courtyard and cannons situated on each end to protect the "human cargo" that colonial countries benefited by free forced labor. Many scenes from the underground hit movie, Sankofa, were shot at the Cape Coast Dungeon.

Former President Rawlings presented a bill proposal to grant Dual Citizenship to those African-Americans and other Blacks in the diaspora which was designed to make them citizens of Ghana and wherever they are currently living requiring no visa for entry. President Barack Obama's first trip to Africa as American Head of State was in Ghana, where he took his family to visit the slave dungeons on the coast along with other diplomatic responsibilities he wanted to accomplished there. President Obama's father was a native of Kenya where many of his relatives still live, including his paternal grandmother at the time of his visit. Ghana's shining black star is a guiding light for all people of African descent in the Diaspora to come back home.

Haiti and Dominican Republic:
Hispaniola, An Island Of Contrasts

By Rolling Out | November 4, 2014

2ⁿᵈ Largest Island in the Caribbean: Hispaniola

My trip to the Dominican Republic and Haiti was something I had been looking forward to for some time as I arrived on the island Hispaniola, formerly Española, part of the Greater Antilles archipelago, now divided by these two republics in the Caribbean region. European nations competed for control of this island in the New World, in the Caribbean as well as in North America. France and Spain settled their hostilities on this island by the Treaty of Ryswick in 1697 and divided Hispaniola between them. As a gateway to the Caribbean, Hispaniola became a haven for pirates during the early colonial period. Both Haiti and the Dominican Republic remain stark contrasts to each other, residing on one island with two distinct cultures and traditions that has added to differences despite being essential being one people with ethnic variances depending on which side of the island they are located.

I first arrived in the capital city of Santo Domingo on the Dominican Republic portion of my trip, regarded as the oldest European city in the New World that has a population of one million residents and an obvious Spanish colonial splendor. Having read about the Dominican Republic many years ago, I had this image of a classic "Banana Republic" with its tropical allure and melting pot population which did not make me deviate from my previous perceptions. Santo Domingo traffic is some of the most congested I have ever seen with horns blaring along streets lined with palm trees, a nice ocean breeze and a Third World charm.

Santo Domingo was the seat of Spanish rule in the Caribbean reflected in the many cathedrals, forts and Spanish colonial icons around the city. Christopher Columbus, who arrived on Dec. 5, 1492, during the first of his four voyages to the Americas, claimed the land for Spain and named it La Espanola. Columbus' older brother, Bartholomew, "founded" the capital city of Santo Domingo around 1496. Slavery was one of the bedrocks of this colonial economy based upon cattle ranching or beef producing plantation economy with a free labor force that was treated less antagonistic than a sugar producing slave economy as in Haiti where antagonism and treatment was more extreme. In cattle ranching, the "master" and "slave" both rode horses and had to work in unison which developed somewhat of a different relationship between black and white, resulting in a lot of race-mixing in the Dominican Republic that is reflected in the faces of all hues of Dominicans. Though some Dominicans recognize their connection to Africa, most look to Spain as the mother country creating a culture of "Hispanicity" especially evident during the era of President Rafael Trujillo (1930-1961); a cruel mulatto dictator who promoted all things related to the "Spanish" way of life and displayed an anti-Haitian sentiment. The Dominican Republic celebrates its independence from Haiti not Spain due to Haiti's 20-year occupation starting in 1822 and ethnic cultural differences that had a profound impact on Dominican national identity.

The people of the Dominican Republic are a spectrum of varied colors — a true rainbow coalition. They are a wonderful, vibrant Spanish speaking people who seem to enjoy the simple things in life such as family time, enjoying beach time at the various places around town like city beach Boca

Chica; the tourists enjoy exclusive resorts in places like Punta Cana and excursions to an isolated Playa Rincon Beach. One of my favorite dishes to try in DR was Sancocho — a meat and vegetable stew indigenous to the Dominican Republic. I also tried a dish that has a direct African origin called Mondongo, a beef tripe soup with a mangu or mashed, boiled plantain also known as fufu. The landscape of the Dominican Republic is absolutely beautiful and made me understand why the Dominican Republic is one the most visited destinations in the Caribbean. I also stayed at the Barcelo Bavaro Beach Resort in Punta Cana for a few days and though I have traveled all over the world, I must say this was the best staff, facility, food, nightly shows, shopping areas and beach that I have ever been to. Special thanks to Martha Martinez (wait staff) and Rafael (bellboy) with Barcelo Bavaro Beach Resort –Adult only section who took care of my every need, Olga Vargas of Amstar for the tours and especially Nacho and Martin of Bavaro Runners Tour Company in Punta Cana.

Departing the Dominican Republic for Haiti, I felt mixed emotions. On one hand, I felt great Black pride in Haiti's triumphant Black revolutionary past as the first Black colony in the new world to have a successful "slave" uprising that liberated itself from their former French colonial masters, but on the other hand I thinking about the devastation of the 7.0 earthquake in 2010 and the overwhelming poverty after the quake. Haiti was already the poorest country in the Western Hemisphere, in part due to 1 billion dollars paid to France for recognition as an independent country that bankrupted the Treasury and some corrupt leaders. Two hundred twenty thousand Haitians lost their lives during the earthquake that also left one and half million homeless but Haitians showed the same resiliency displayed by Haiti's Founding Fathers in establishing the 1st Black Republic in the "New World" with the beautiful universally hued, resilient French Creole speaking Haitians today as they persevere in trying times. Haiti is the birthplace of the Black experience in the Americas with a current population of 10.4 million.

My interest in going to Cap Haitian was because this was the birthplace of what would become the Haitian Revolution and the monuments of Haiti's black generals and leaders can be seen throughout this wonderful city. There I also enjoyed dishes like the classic Haitian patty made of ground beef, salt cod, smoked herring, chicken and ground turkey accompanied by Haitian spices and Du riz a sauce-pois- rice with bean sauce. Cap Haitien was not affected as much as Haiti's capital, Port au Prince during the earthquake in 2010. In Cap Haitien, you don't see the European colonizers on display like in the Dominican Republic but Black Men who defeated the French in war to end slavery and colonization.

I remember reading about Haitian General Toussaint L' Overture many years ago, who was a former slave that became leader of the Haitian

Revolution. He was a military genius whose political acumen transformed an entire country of enslaved blacks into what would become the independent state of Haiti. Though under his leadership at the time, Haiti was still recognized as a colony of France but was free of slavery. The French tricked L 'Overture by kidnaping him during a diplomatic meeting between the two countries and transporting him to prison in France where he would die two years later. However, L 'Overture paved the way for his successor Jean Jacques Dessalines — both were former slaves — who would go on to defeat the French in a war that shook the institution of slavery throughout the world. The historical monuments to Dessalines and others located in Vertiere near Cap Haitien were impressive and the Citadel, built by Dessalines' successor Henri Christophe with 20,000 men, was awe-inspiring. No foreign invader would ever test the walls of the Citadel.

On Jan. 1, 1804, Dessalines would declare Haiti's Independence with this momentous statement for any future aggression by France to re-colonize Haiti and reinstate slavery, "Let them tremble when they approach our coast, if not for the memories of the atrocities they perpetrated here but from the terrible resolution we will have made to put to death anyone born French, whose profane foot soils the Land of Liberty". Much of the world would not initially recognize Haiti's independence and US President Thomas Jefferson called Haiti's revolutionary heroes, "Cannibals of the Terrible

Republic" simply because Black men defeated their white colonial masters in war. Special thanks to Kenneth Kwame Welsh of Atlanta Segments of Welsh Information Services LLC for the Haitian technical support. What a journey of discovery for me to visit both of these two wonderful countries in contrast on the Isle of Hispaniola.

Mandela's South Africa
By Rolling Out | February 8, 2014

Montage Of Me In South Africa

In reflecting on the recent passing of the iconic Nelson Mandela or as he is affectionately called Madiba, I think of what South Africa was like during Apartheid, during his Presidency and what the future is for Mandela's South Africa. I visited South Africa in 1996 and had well prepared myself for what to expect having read Nelson Mandela's book, Long Walk to Freedom, as well as other books like Steven Biko's book, I Write What I Like, along with Kaffir Boy by Mark Mathabene which left such an indelible upon me years earlier as I thought about Apartheid in South Africa and compared it to Jim Crow segregation here in the United States. It amazed me that I was visiting South Africa a mere 2 years after apartheid ended with the election of Nelson Mandela in 1994 but I did not permit myself to harbor any delusions of grandeur about the continued need for struggle in the Republic of South Africa as my departure time to Johannesburg, South Africa approached. As I boarded my connecting flight in Cairo, Egypt, thoughts seemed to constantly resonate in my mind about my prior study of the South African struggle and contrasted by the historical struggle of the Black man and woman in America was coming to be fulfilled in the comparative reality or post-apartheid South Africa. Names like Steven Biko, Nelson and Winnie Mandela, David and Elizabeth Sibeko, Archbishop Desmond Tutu, Chief Albert Lutuli , Chris Hani, the Sharpsville Massacre, the Soweto Uprising and countless other people and events began to dominate my thoughts as I patiently waited for the 8 hour flight to be complete.

One of the most impactful events for me was the Sharpsville Massacre on March 21, 1960, which marked a turning point for South African Blacks with the murder of 60 black protestors, along with 178 wounded when the Pan Africanist Congress (PAC) organized a passbook protest at the Sharpsville Tennis Court grounds. The passbook or passbook law required Africans to carry these passbooks, similar to a passport that has to be stamped, at all times when traveling throughout South Africa during Apartheid. The National Party, the ruling political party during Apartheid, had the Riot Squad dispatched at these grounds and opened fire upon these unarmed protestors with at least 80% being shot in the back as they retreated. Another event that I thought about was the Soweto Uprising, when African school children protested having to learn the oppressor's Afrikaans language (Dutch, Boer, Germanic origin) on June 16, 1976 where many of these children were massacred as they ran away from being fired upon. The first place I visited in South Africa after arrival was the memorial erected for the children killed in front of the South African police station where the gathered to protest. One of the first children killed, 13 year old Hector Peterson, was photographed by a reporter where his limp body was carried away by another child running in one of the most infamous photographs ever taken during that era. The spirit of the children resisting will always be remembered for generations with the memorial erected that has the bold inscription: "Never, Never Again"!

As I traveled with Bongaini Sibeko, the son of slain PAC revolutionary David Sibeko, I saw that the struggle was not over for our people there because a critical element was not implemented by the African National Congress – a radical redistribution of wealth to help the oppressed Black masses. I also had the honor of meeting Bongaini's mother, Elizabeth Sibeko, who I spoke with on many occasions along with Khoison X who was the Secretary General of the Pan Africanist Congress and one of the most feared political men in South Africa. As we traveled throughout the countryside, I witnessed the masses living below what we would call poverty in America as we went in places like Soweto (Southwestern Township) in these shanty towns that literally went for miles and miles. It was easy for me to draw some obvious conclusions, but I can understand the diplomacy exhibited by the ANC to be careful about a minority white uprising if this redistribution took place, even though I disagreed in light of the radical oppression of Black South Africans by criminal settlers that showed no humanity for years of minority white rule. The ANC aim seemed to be that to hold the country in harmony and seeking unity for all South Africans to precedence over any form of reparations. Imagining the pressure on Mandela and the ANC was a stark reality pill I had to swallow despite the fact that I felt "white folks" still controlled the wealth and land of South Africa. Since

I was not living there and could draw an easy conclusion coming from America, which is the world's number one superpower, my radical way of thinking was a luxury I could afford to have since I had a return ticket back to the USA. My love and respect for Nelson Mandela and the ANC will never dissipate, even though I was more attracted to the PAC, which had a more radical political aim than the ANC. I felt at the time that to fly a new flag was not good enough when the masses of Black South Africans lived in poverty.

Eighty-seven percent of the most fertile land in South Africa belonged to six white ruling families, including the Openhiemers and DeBeers, who run the gold and diamond industries there respectively. Given many of these historical events, I could not believe how beautiful South Africa was as I traveled between Johannesburg and Cape Town, a two hour flight at the tip of South Africa where I thought my plane came pretty close to the picturesque Table Mountain for my comfort. In Cape Town, I saw Robben Island where Nelson Mandela would spend the bulk of his 27 years in prison and understood his sentiments in his book Long Walk to Freedom and how he and his comrades would remain steadfast in their commitment to a united South Africa verses Apartheid. I truly admire them for the conviction they showed over the years. I admired that and was riveted to the television when I saw him released from prison on February 11, 1990 having been sentenced in 1964. Just hours after his release he told a roaring crowd, "Today, the majority of South

Africans, black and white, recognize that apartheid has no future. It has to be ended by our decisive mass action. We have waited too long for our freedom". To see him become President of a new South Africa in 1994 sent chills through my body and filled with pride that at least the Apartheid system, like Jim Crow, was a thing of the past , though the remnants still remained in various forms. While much can still be said for the majority of Black South Africans living in poverty, many will point out that the Black Middle Class has soared and is rapidly growing. According to Stellenbosch University in Johannesburg, the county's black middle class has grown from 350,000 people in 1993 to around 3 million in 2012. This study concluded with a statement by research fellow Hennie Kotze who said, "That is not to justify the pace of change, but rather to dispel possible misconceptions fueled by recent evidence of social fragmentation and racial tensions". The study also concluded that while affluent black people have higher income levels, they still have fewer assets than their white counterparts.

I would later understand the wisdom of Nelson Mandela and others in the ANC who realized that this social revolution is indeed a process, not a conclusion. Preparing to depart Azania, the indigenous name of South Africa, I realized that you can call it Apartheid or Jim Crow but we are truly connected to our brothers and sisters in South Africa through struggle and want the best for each other. There is an African proverb that says, "Polluted

Waters will cleanse itself, as long as it keeps running"; so Nelson Mandela's long walk to freedom has concluded but it will be up to the current leaders of South Africa, including current President Jacob Zuma, to continue this walk Nelson started toward freedom but reciprocity to the poor and masses of Black South Africans- Rest well Madiba.

Secrets To A Long Life From Supercentenarian Josephine Guy, 111
By Rolling Out | February 3, 2015

Golden Aunt Jo

There's nothing more refreshing on a hot day in the Bayou than a glass of lemonade and a slice of cake in a small town to celebrate the birthday of a centenarian. When Friday, July 23, 2010, was proclaimed "Josephine Guy" day in Zachary, Louisiana, by then-Mayor Henry Martinez marking a major milestone, it was the 106th anniversary of the Bank of Zachary and its oldest customer, Josephine Guy, was also 106 years old at the time.

Born in 1904, this past Jan. 4, Guy celebrated her 111th birthday, making her one of the oldest living persons in the U.S. Misao Okawa of Japan is currently the oldest living person in the world. She will turn 116 on March 5, 2015.

A mother of six, with a host of grandchildren, great grands and great great grands, Guy was born in Mississippi but spent most of her life in Baywood, Louisiana, in the northeast corner of East Baton Rouge Parish.

Aunt Josephine And Aunt Daisy

A great-nephew, Malik Ismail, is in awe of his great aunts, including Guy's younger sister, Daisy Anderson Square, 90, who he says are "going on strong."

A lover of sports, with her favorite song being "Play Ball Boys," she's lived a healthy life and remained very active in her garden until she turned 100. According to Ismail, Aunt Josephine's tips to longevity are:

1. Keep God first.
2. Cherish family.
3. Don't eat your food out of a can.

At press time, rolling out received correspondence that Josephine Anderson Guy passed away peacefully on Monday, Feb. 2, 2015.

Ismail cherishes her memory, "What a life she lived at 111years-old! What her eyes have seen ... My Aunt Everlasting."

Slavery And Reparations: Roles Played By Presidents, Founding Fathers (Pt.1)

By Rolling Out | November 23, 2013

(Photo courtesy Malik Ismail)

According to *Webster's Dictionary*, a criminal is one who has committed a crime or a person who has been convicted of a crime – a rapist, murderer, robber or thief. Criminal judgments can be passed on an individual or collective. Few would deny that America and Europe have been by far the world's greatest criminals and the proof is marked by historical data. Among the greatest crimes committed by America and Europe is the institution of slavery and colonization. The European and American Slave Trade was the most brutal, inhuman institution ever brought on a people and Africans were the primary victims of this holocaust, which lasted over 400 years and continues to plague people of African descent to this day.

The African Holocaust of 100 million must never be forgotten by black people in Africa and America because of the impact it has had on our people in the way we view ourselves, how others view us and the mental shackles that remain the everpresent reminder of a traumatic past.

In America, we have a well-documented history of slave-owning leaders including the "Founding Fathers" and early Presidents, who indulged in the American Slave Trade for forced "free" labor. Here is a partial list:

1. George Washington, America's first President, owned 216 slaves in 1771.

2. Patrick "Give me liberty or give me death" Henry, owned 65 slaves at the time of his death.

3. Andrew Jackson owned 160 slaves during his term as Commander in Chief.

4. James K. Polk, the 11th President, owned 18 slaves.

5. Thomas Jefferson owned 185 slaves in 1809.

6. Abraham Lincoln, the so-called Great Emancipator, said during a debate in 1858, "I, as much as any other man, am in favor of having a Superior position assigned to the White race."

7. Ulysses S. Grant owned 4 slaves.

8. Theodore Roosevelt, the 26th President, in a letter to a friend wrote, "Now as to the Negroes, I entirely agree with you that as a race and mass, they are altogether inferior to whites."

(In part 2, the author discusses what Blacks are owed by European and American colonizers).

Slavery and Reparations: Who's responsible for this crime against humanity? (Pt.2)

By Rolling Out | November 23, 2013

Malik Ismail In Cape Coast Slave Dungeon In Ghana West

African Where Many Africans Exited The Door Of No Return To Never See Mother Africa Again.

Black people in Africa and America must indeed convict America and Europe for the crimes committed during the African Holocaust. After conviction, a punishment and fine must be carried out against the guilty parties. In the sphere of punishment for America and Europe, there needs to be recognition of the crime, atonement, reparations and then reconciliation.

History has always proven to be best qualified to reward all research and the fact that both America and Europe owe Black people preparations for the crimes committed against the sons and daughters of Africa at home and abroad. The overwhelming question is: what does America owe the descendants of those who were taken from Africa, in turn robbing Africa of its greatest resource–its people?

America has the nerve to support other countries in a welfare position such as Israel, sending $4-6 billion annually, and setting up a Holocaust museum on this soil financing the operating expenses but nothing is offered to Black people who suffered under white supremacy for over 400 years. The United States spent billions to pave a way for "democracy" in Russia, but practices hypocrisy when it comes to its former slaves.

What does Europe owe our Black brothers and sisters who are still being exploited and robbed of the mineral wealth of the African soil where many are forced to work for little or nothing? Exploiters like the DeBeers of South Africa continue to economically exploit our people and are the benefactors of a criminal settler colony in the midst of "native indigenous people" just like Israel, Australia and America.

No amount will ever pay for the effects the African Holocaust has had upon Black people but these criminals can start to atone by giving our people a true share of the land, wealth and IMF debit elimination that has in turn helped these countries become so rich and powerful at our expense.

"I have no mercy or pity in me for a country that will crush a people, and then penalize them for not being able to stand up under the weight" – Malcolm X, 1964

(In part 3, the author delves deeper into the topic of colonialism, which birthed capitalism and summarizes how we seek reparations).

Slavery And Reparations: Prison Industrial Complex Is A Profitable Enterprise (Pt.3)
By Rolling Out | November 23, 2013

If you force a person to work for you free of charge for just a week, you will make a profit, then make 1,000 people work for free an entire year, you will become wealthy but imagine forcing over 100 million people of African ancestry to work free of charge for 400 years. America is the No. 1 superpower in the world today because the bedrock of its wealth was derived from the free labor of enslaved Africans and their descendants. The United States is unquestionably the mightiest government on Earth...the mightiest, the richest and the wickedest. No one can deny that America's wealth and power stems from 400 years of slave labor and Europe has been the great benefactor of tremendous wealth and power from the darker people of the world, especially in Africa.

In fact, all over Earth the British have colonized indigenous people through force and violence against dark nations. In China during the Opium Wars or the Boxer Rebellion in the early 1800s, the British white man dumped tons of addictive opium into China and when the Chinese rebelled against this proliferation of this drug in their country, they were militarily defeated. By 1837, so many Chinese became Opium addicts that it was perceived that one-third of the population was addicted. Imagine this, the British white man declared war on the Chinese because they resisted the drugs coming in their country. Generation after generation of opium addicts were created by the British, who after defeating the Chinese, put signs on their buildings that read, " No Dogs or Chinese allowed." Black America experienced a similar fate by having crack cocaine being flooded into our communities, which reached epidemic proportions.

The No. 1 growth industry in America is the Prison Industrial Complex, which has made a profitable enterprise out of human suffering, especially as it relates to drug abuse perpetrated by this very system. For example, 20 years ago there were 19,000 prisons in America; today there are over 124,000 prisons. A commodity is being made of Black and Brown communities, who continue to suffer from self-hatred, negative media images and social ostracism. The criminal justice system established an unbalanced judicial penalty during the crack epidemic by having a person caught with five grams of crack cocaine for a first time nonviolent offense receive a 5-year mandatory sentence. For 500 grams of powder cocaine, you can receive probation. Although numbers of crack cocaine users have increased for poor whites, 94 percent of crack cocaine users were still Black and Brown people. And 75 percent of powder cocaine users were white males. The "criminal" criminal justice system has targeted low income Black and Brown people. Black people today are the victims of a literal "slave" system and "slave" mentality that continues to permeate in a country that had no use for us after slavery.

Reparations is a debt that is owed to Black people in America and Africa- where the remnants of colonialism has been replaced by neo-colonialism in many African countries , thus taking on the nature and characteristics of their former colonial masters. Native Americans, Japanese interned in concentration camps and others have received some forms of Reparations for what they went through, but what about Black people in America, who unlike these other people, were robbed of any connection to their indigenous culture in Africa. This long overdue debt must be collected with the demand of our collective unity. Public opinion and historical education is the key. Let us make this command together-worldwide.

The Father Of Black History Month: Dr. Carter G. Woodson By Rolling Out | February 8, 2014

Carter G. Woodson (Photo courtesy of Malik Ismail)

In order to understand the importance of Black History Month, we all need to learn about the founder of what began as Negro History Week and would later evolve to become Black History Month by the great scholar, historian and educator Dr. Carter G. Woodson. The yearly celebration of Black History Month in February is directly attributed to Dr. Woodson, who was born to parents that were former slaves in Kentucky on December 19, 1875, five years after the 15th Amendment to the Constitution was passed granting Blacks the right to vote which happened to be the same month the first Black U.S. Senator named Hiram R. Revels (1822-1901) took his oath of office. Carter spent his early years working in the Kentucky coal mines and enrolled in high school at age twenty. He graduated in two years and later went on to earn a doctorate from Harvard University. The scholar was disturbed to find in his studies that history books largely ignored the Black American population and when Blacks did figure into the picture, it was generally in ways that reflected the inferior social position they were assigned at that time as he desired to champion the "innovative culture" people of African descent developed in America after the long separation from their "traditional culture" in Africa which was his way of responding to this cultural crisis.

Always one to act on his ambitions, Woodson decided to take the challenge of writing Black Americans into the nation's history. He established the Association for the Study of Negro Life and History in 1915 and a year later founded the widely respected Journal of Negro History. In February 1926, Woodson launched Negro History Week as an initiative to bring national attention to the contributions of Black people throughout American society. The "whitewashing" of history in America has negatively impacted African-Americans and their image of themselves in the world. There remained a vital need to correct the misinformation of our achievements which became his life's work. Woodson chose the second week of February for Negro History Week because it marks the birthdays of two men who greatly influenced him and the Black population then, Frederick Douglas and U.S. President Abraham Lincoln. However, February has much more than Douglas and Lincoln to show for its significance in Black American history. Woodson, influenced by early Black scholar pioneer J.A. Rogers, would inspire the likes of John Henrik Clarke, Dr. Cheikh Ante Diop, Ivan van Sertima, Dr. Frances Cres Welsing, Dr. Yosef Ben-Jochannan, Dr. Chancellor Williams, Anthony Browder, John Hope Franklin and many others.

Carter G. Woodson's Book (Photo courtesy of Malik Ismail)

Americans have recognized Black History Month annually for 87 years, but before this was established, black history had barely begun to be studied or even documented when the tradition originated. Although Blacks have been in America at least as far back as colonial times, it was not until the 20th century that they gained a respectable presence in the history books. Woodson provided a ray of reality in the midst of distortion and provided a wonderful opportunity recognize our people's accomplishments through a week then month's focus. All mature people around the world celebrate themselves in some form or fashion and Woodson recognized championing the created innovative culture we developed here would be Woodson wrote the great and illuminating book, *The Mis-Education of the Negro,* in 1933, which showed how concurrent negative images affected Blacks in how we were viewed by others and most importantly, how we view ourselves. Later in the 1940s, Black psychologists Kenneth and Mamie Clark used the "Doll Test" to determine how Black children viewed race when they had to choose between a black doll and a white doll, where they overwhelmingly picked the white doll as the most desired and beautiful for them to play with. When asked to describe the black doll, they said it was bad and ugly, showing the psychological damage done by social and systematic racism. In the 2005 documentary "Girl like Me" by Kiri Davis, who was then 16 years old, duplicated this experiment for 21st century and found that 15 out of the twenty children preferred the white or light-skinned doll when asked to pick the "nice doll", showing even today that black kids know what they are taught to value and it is not them. This makes Woodson's Black History Month more important than ever to study not just in February, but every day and we are eternally grateful to him for his contribution. Dr. Carter G. Woodson died April 3, 1950, but left a lasting gift to his people. A quote from Dr. Woodson, "When you control a man's thinking, you do not have to worry about his actions. You do not have to tell him not to stand here or go yonder. He will find his 'proper place' and will stay in it. You do not need to send him to the back door. He will go without being told. In fact, if there is no back door, he will cut one for his special benefit. His education makes it necessary."

Meet the Author

Malik Ismail (born as James Robinson, Jr. on August 24, 1965) is an international writer and revolutionary activist born in Miami, Florida. Ismail is one of three siblings with his sister, Mia Robinson, and half-brother, Jai Harris. He is married to Kathy Ismail-Robinson. Ismail's parents, James Robinson, Sr. and Vera Anderson Robinson, are both deceased. From an early age Malik Ismail was influenced by Malcom X, Muhammad Ali and the Black Panther

Party, which would impact his life in activism. Malik also had an uncle named Ulas Hayes who was a civil rights icon in Baton Rouge, Louisiana, where his mother's side of the family resided. He had a high regard for his Uncle Ulas, along with his grandfather, Jarrot Anderson, Sr.

As an international traveler, historian and writer Malik has explored many cultures in Africa, including Ghana, South Africa, Egypt as well as other places he visited like Cuba, Rio de Janeiro and Salvador Bahia, Brazil including the favelas of Rocinha and Cidade de Dues (City of God.) Recent trips to the Dominican Republic and Haiti would inspire him to write about his experiences with the people there, particularly those of African descent. A former Panther Minister of Information IRU the New Panther Vanguard Movement (formerly known as New African-American Vanguard Movement) whose writings have been published in *The L.A. Watts Times*, *rolling out* Magazine, *It's About Time* newsletter, *The Black Panther International News Service,* and he has been profiled in *The African Times*. Ismail is an Honorary Member of the 1976-1981 Southern California Chapter of the Black Panther Party.

Listed below are a few highlights of Malik Ismail's life:

August 1994: Malik Ismail went to Africa visiting Egypt and Ghana, West Africa where he found a greater sense of self, especially after meeting Kwame Ture' a.k.a. Stokely Carmichael in Accra, Ghana. While in Ghana, he visited the W.E.B. DuBois Center for Pan-African Studies also in Accra, Ghana. Ismail met Akbar Muhammad, International Representative for the Honorable Minister Louis Farrakhan of the Nation of Islam, along with Ismael Muhammad, son of the Honorable Elijah

Muhammad, and leading members of the Original Hebrew Israelites of Dimona, Israel. Having long admired Malcolm X, Muhammad Ali and the Black Panther Party, he dedicated his life's work to his people and oppressed people of all colors. While on the African continent, he had an opportunity to study the life of Dr. Osageyfo Kwame Nkrumah, Ghana's first post-colonial President. He also studied W.E.B. Dubois, who lived the remaining part of his life in Accra, Ghana. Malik would be inspired to support reparations campaigns after visiting the "slave" dungeons in Elmina and Cape Coast that were the beginning point of the slave trade in Ghana where many Africans were taken from their homeland never to return.

October 1994: After returning from Africa, Malik joined the New African American Vanguard Movement (which was later changed to the New Panther Vanguard Movement), during its inception and married longtime childhood friend, Kathleen LeMelle.

March 1995: Malik was named Minister of Information of the NPVM and was the youngest selected for membership on the Vanguard's Leadership Council. As National Minister of Information, he was the organization's Chief Propagandist and made plans to help re-issue the Black Panther Intercommunal News Service.

June 1995: Malik was chiefly responsible for raising the money to re-establish the Black Panther International News Service in the community. (The title of the paper changed from *Intercommunal* to *International*.) During his Los Angeles tenure, Malik helped create working coalitions with organizations and political parties like the Nation of Islam, the US Organization, the National People's Campaign, the Coalition Against Police Abuse (CAPA), the Latasha Harlins Justice Committee, the Pan-Africanist Congress in South Africa, N-COBRA Reparations Organization, National People's Democratic Uhuru Movement and the Free Fred Hampton, Jr. Campaign.

August 1996: Malik traveled to South Africa as an emissary for the New Panther Vanguard Movement, where he met with Elizabeth and Bongaini Sibeko, widow and son of PanAfricanist Congress leader, David Sibeko, along with meeting with Khoisan X, Secretary General of the Pan-Africanist Congress. He established the short-lived Soweto Mission for the children of Soweto.

May 1997: Malik and Kathleen moved to Atlanta, Georgia where Malik continued to organize for the New Panther Vanguard Movement with the added title of National Eastern Representative of the NPVM. Malik has spoken on platforms with Jesse Jackson, Maxine Waters, Dr. Maulana Karenga, Dr. Khalid Abdul Muhammad and others on various issues as well as college campuses, organizations and rallies. He continued to organize events, food giveaways and Survival programs for the New

Panther Vanguard Movement. Malik's articles have appeared in a variety of newspapers. He has been interviewed by many publications as well as appeared on National Public Radio (NPR), TV shows and radio programs. He has interviewed Akua Njeri (Deborah Johnson), former Chicago Black Panther and fiancé of assassinated Chicago Black Panther Leader Fred Hampton and mother of activist Fred Hampton Jr. Malik also interviewed former Black Panther leader Elaine Brown, both for *The Black Panther International News Service*.

After the New Panther Vanguard Movement disbanded in 2002, Malik Ismail continues to write features on politics, travel, history, culture and activism as well as doing genealogy research on his maternal link to the Fulani tribe in Guinea, West Africa and Mbundu tribe in Angola, Central Africa on his paternal side. In this book, From Old Guard to Vanguard: A Second Generation Panther, the author shares his experiences working with the New Panther Vanguard Movement and the influence that former Black Panther Party members Charles "Boko" Freeman, Shareef Abdullah and B. Kwaku Duren had on him in his development as a revolutionary activist.

Books / Newspaper References for Malik Ismail, NPVM, NAAVM

* Liberation, Imagination and the Black Panther Party by Kathleen Cleaver and George Katsiaficas page 50

* The Black Panther Party Reconsidered by Charles E. Jone page 5,6 & 47

* Newspapers: Pasadena Weekly Black by Popular Demand article by Theresa Moreau page 8

* Articles, features, profiles on Malik Ismail: African Times July 115, 1995 page 3 Profile: The Rebirth of the Black Panthers with New Ideals

  * The Black Panther International New Service Vol. 1 No. 2 Spring 1997 Page 3 Black Leadership: Soldiers or Sellouts? Page 13 South Africa: The Illusion of Freedom

* The Black Panther International News Service Vol. 1 No. 1 Page 6 and 7 Reparations: Prosecuting a Criminal Page 9 Profiles in Black: Lead, Follow or get...Out the Way

* San Diego Union Tribune Monday, January 30, 1995 Page E1 & E3 The Panthers New Path by Shante Morgan, Copley News Service

* L.A. Watts Times August 21, 1997 Vol. XXV, No. 531 View Point section page 2-10 Truth without Justice is Injustice by Malik Ismail

  * It's About Time special issue Vol. 5, No. 4 , pg 20 Chickens Always come home to Roost by Malik Ismail

The Black Panther International News Service Vol. 1, No. 4 Page 6 Malik Ismail interviews Akua Njeri - former Chicago BPP member and fiancé of assassinated BPP Chicago leader Fred Hampton and page 19 Ghana: Black Shining Star by Malik Ismail , pg. 20 Propaganda for the Soul , Programs for the Body by Malik Ismail

The Black Panther Intercommunal News Service Vol. 1, No. 7 , Autumn 2000 Letters section, page 5 Protracted Struggle vs Spontaneous Struggle by Malik Ismail

The Black Panther International News Service, Vol. 1, No. 3 Summer 1997 Page 8 & 12 Truth without Justice is Injustice by Malik Ismail

L.A. Watts Times February 27, 1997 Vol. XVV , No. 505 Page 2 View Point section. South Africa: The Illusion of Freedom by Malik Ismail

L.A. Watts Times Vol. XVIII , 445 1996 Page 8-9 NAAVM , US Organization Unite in Kwanzaa " Umoja " Observation & Rolling Out Los Angeles Power Movement: The Black Panther Party for Self Defense

"Bunchy" Carter   **John Huggins**

Photo courtesy of The Black Panther International News Service

Alprentice "Bunchy" Carter and John Huggins of the Southern California Chapter of the Black Panther Party assassinated January 17, 1969 at UCLA. Bunchy and John are martyrs for both the L.A. Black Panthers and the Panther Vanguard Movement who emerged in the 90s to continue the work of our first generation comrades. The Southern California chapter was the most decimated chapter in the entire Black Panther Party with the murder of Black Panthers

My Fallen Comrades in the New Panther Vanguard Movement:

Top left, Sister Pat (L.A.); top right, Loretta Dillon (IND); bottom left Hanif Mack (L.A.) and bottom right, Vanguard co-founder and original BPP member Shareef Abdullah – Rest in Peace and Power.

Historic 50th Anniversary Black Panther Photo Shoot at Alameda County Courthouse Steps in Oakland, California October 23, 2016

FROM OLD GUARD TO VANGUARD:
A SECOND GENERATION PANTHER

"Comrade Malik Ismail tells the story of the New Panther Vanguard Movement, the only legitimate heir to the reigns of the original Black Panther Party as led by longtime activist B. Kwaku Duren" - Kato *"Gato"* Cooks, member of the Southern California Chapter of the Black Panther Party.

"The Black Panther Party did not stop in the 80s, the Black Panther Newspaper did not stop in the 80s, NPVM is part of our legacy in the Black Panther Party, Right on NPVM" - Bill Jennings, Black Panther Party Commemorate Committee

"The L.A. Panthers (NPVM) are on target" - Bobby Seale, cofounder of the Black Panther Party, quoted in the Pasadena Weekly (July 16, 1998)

CPSIA information can be obtained
at www.ICGtesting.com
Printed in the USA
LVHW080413230421
685319LV00021B/321